ESSENTIAL
GREECE
TRAVEL GUIDE

Your Complete Tourist information to help you explore like a Pro

Adam J. Scott

2025

COPYRIGHTS

LEGAL DISCLAIMER!

Table of Contents

From the Author

Who doesn't want to visit Greece? Hardly will you find any travel enthusiast who doesn't have Greece on their checklist.

But like a domino, this is all boils down to making the most of your visit when you are now ready to embark on it.

Greece is full! The country is brimming, and overflowing with what will make every heart and soul drool. Talk of history, talk of culture, talk of stories, of all sorts. In Greece you will find it all. Why go on to talk about it when you are going to see it all in here.

The perfect guide to Greece 2025 is here. Take it all in. Your Tour Guide is ready!

Kalosorisma!

Chapter One

All about Greece

Greece is the country that had some of the oldest civilizations in this world but is so much a part of the twenty first century as well. Majestic islands, long sandy coasts, historical heritage, warm wonderful weather it is still the paradises that retains the fascination. Where the history enthusiasts, the food lovers and those, who want to spend time on a sea shore, will find something to do.

Historical Timeline of Greece

- **C. 800 BC – Ancient Greece begins:** The rise of Greek city-states like Athens, Sparta, and Corinth. Foundations of Western civilization, philosophy, democracy, and mythology laid down.

- **C. 776 BC – First Olympic Games:** Held in Olympia, marking the start of the traditional Greek Olympic Games.

- **C. 508 BC – Birth of Democracy:** Cleisthenes introduces the first democratic system in Athens.

- **490 BC – 479 BC – Greco-Persian Wars:** Greeks, led by Athens and Sparta, defeat the Persian Empire in battles like Marathon and Salamis.

- **C. 447 BC – 432 BC – Construction of the Parthenon:** The iconic temple is built during the height of Athens' Golden Age under Pericles.

- **431 BC – 404 BC – Peloponnesian War:** A major conflict between Athens and Sparta, ending with Spartan victory and weakening of Athens.

- **336 BC – 323 BC – Alexander the Great's reign:** King of Macedonia, Alexander creates one of the largest empires in history, spreading Greek culture across Europe, Asia, and North Africa.

- 146 BC – Greece becomes part of the Roman Empire: Rome conquers Greece, though Greek culture continues to influence Roman life.

- C. 330 AD – Byzantine Empire begins: Greece becomes part of the Eastern Roman Empire, with Constantinople as its capital.

- C. 1204 AD – Fourth Crusade: Crusaders sack Constantinople, leading to the fragmentation of the Byzantine Empire and control by Western powers in parts of Greece.

- 1453 AD – Fall of Constantinople: Marks the end of the Byzantine Empire and beginning of Ottoman rule over Greece.

- 1453 – 1821 AD – Ottoman Rule: Greece remains under Ottoman Empire control for nearly 400 years, though Greek culture and religion continue to survive.

- 1821 – 1830 AD – Greek War of Independence: After years of struggle, Greece gains independence from the Ottoman Empire, officially recognized in 1830.

- 1832 AD – Kingdom of Greece established: Greece becomes a monarchy with King Otto of Bavaria as its first king.

- **1912 – 1913 AD – Balkan Wars:** Greece gains additional territory, including Thessaloniki, after successful campaigns against the Ottoman Empire.

- **1940 – 1944 AD – World War II:** Greece is invaded by Axis forces, leading to German occupation. Greece plays a significant role in resisting the Axis powers.

- **1946 – 1949 AD – Greek Civil War:** A conflict between government forces and communist insurgents, leading to the establishment of a Western-aligned government.

- **1974 AD – Abolishment of the monarchy:** Greece transitions into a parliamentary republic following the collapse of a military junta.

- **1981 AD – Greece joins the European Union:** Greece becomes part of the European Economic Community (now the EU), marking its integration into Europe.

- **2004 AD – Athens hosts the Olympic Games:** The modern Olympics return to their birthplace after more than a century.

- **2009 – 2018 AD – Greek Debt Crisis:** A major financial crisis hits Greece, leading to economic austerity measures and reforms supported by the EU and IMF.

- **2020s – Modern Greece:** Greece emerges from the economic crisis with a focus on tourism, culture, and innovation, continuing to preserve its rich historical legacy.

Historic Places in Greece to Explore

Greece is still rich in ancient sites and ageless monuments, thru places that tour guides would always boast as sight-seeing attractions. No matter you are just strolling in Athens streets or going hiking in a secluding island or exploring the beautiful countryside, you will come across history at every corner. Be it the large palaces and theaters or the small ruins and Byzantine churches, everything in the country has something interesting to tell. In the following list check out these mind blowing historical places that you should never miss to visit.

The Acropolis of Athens

However, we need to start with the Acropolis as it is the icon of Ancient Greece, isn't it? This is a historical fortification located in the central part of Athens on the hill that has been built at the 5th century BC. The creation that is most emblematic of Doric architecture is the Parthenon, an edifice also called the temple of Athena, the patroness and the symbol of wisdom.

It is quite possible to spend considerable amount of time strolling around, admiring the view of contemporary Athens beneath as well as trying to picture the atmosphere of the city when such prominent philosophers as Socrates used to walk here. The best thing about the Acropolis is that it is not only a historical landmark to visit but also it is quite possible to think about today's world from the perspective of the past. But be sure to also visit the New Acropolis Museum for a closer look of the artefacts recovered from the site.

Delphi

But if you are interested in mythology or simply intrigued by the enigma of the ancient civilizations – Delphi is a place for you. In ancient times this was known as 'the navel of the earth' by the Greeks because of the great Temple of Apollo on the site, the Oracle of Delphi.

The tourist attraction that may be of interest here includes the Temple of Apollo which has great columns and sits against the backdrop of the mountain. Indeed it is easy to understand why it was believed to be as magical as it was considered by many. As one moves around the areas where the structures used to be you can almost imagine it in your nose. Just 90 minutes away is the Delphi Archaeological Museum that contains such masterpieces as the Charioteer of Delphi that does not fails to impress even today.

Ancient Olympia

Do you love sports? If you have the time you would not want to miss the Ancient Olympia – the birth place of Olympic Games in 776BC. This place was once home to many structures including the temples, the exercising ground for athletes and the stadium where the athletes performed. Admiring the remains of the stadium today, one can easily imagine the sound of people shouting for their favourite contenders in the past. They have remnants of the Temple of Zeus one of the seven wonders of the ancient world or in this case what is left of it.

However, there is still a lot to offer for tourists like the original Olympic track and the Philippeio, a round shaped building which constructed by King Philip II of Macedon. It would therefore be advised to walk round the Olympia Archaeological Museum in order to get a full appreciation of the site's multi-faceted role in sport and religion.

The Palace of Knossos

One of the most mysterious archaeological areas located on Crete which is the largest island of Greece is the Palace of Knossos. This monument is a palace which also belongs to the Minoan civilization that existed around 2000 BC and it is among the oldest cultures in Europe.

According to ancient Greek mythology this is the place where the world's first labyrinth was built, to house the half-man half-bull monster: the Minotaur. There is a considerably large number of reliefs, frescoes, throne rooms, and gigantic pithoi that were used in storing olive oil and wine in the region. The palace is large, and having walked through that part I too felt that maze like setting chosen for constructing the story of the Labyrinth fits well.

Meteora

Greek Meteora is what one can safely think of as a fairytale place. Sitting in central Greece this place is known for its massive rocks and on top of which are six monasteries which are still in use. The name Meteora literally translates as 'suspended in the air'; and when you look at these monasteries standing atop rough cliffs you will know why.

These monasteries were constructed between the 14th and 16th centuries, although many more were originally furnished across the region; there are now only a few which continue to function. There are well-trodden trails of steeps and stairs that have been made of stones which lead you up to these caves, and at the top you will be able to sight the views of the surrounding terrains. The monasteries houses contain paintings which date back to hundreds of years, and book that have been written down in manuscripts and moreover there is tranquility in Meteora, appropriate for those who like to meditate.

Mycenae

Travel back in time even more to the Mycenae that served as among the oldest city-states in the Greek history and famous for legends. There is a story that Mycenae was the home of king Agamemnon, the leader of Greeks during the war of Troy. The walls of the city are Cyclopean walls and the stones used were so massive that it could only have been worked by Cyclops.

When you cross the Lion Gate through which a visitor enters the city you truly feel historical presence. Do not leave Mycenae without visiting at least the Treasury of Atreus – it is a beehive shaped tomb, which looks surprisingly modern – or the Archaeological Museum of Mycenae which will please visitors with stunning gold Death masks and swords or any other weapon, aged several thousand years. He even took care of beautifying the temple that is situated in Sounion and dedicated to Poseidon.

Just 30 km southeast of Attica, the Temple of Poseidon at Cape Sounion is the perfect place for the EVEREST 2012 winners: private, magnificent views and ancient history.

This is situated about an hour's drive away from the capital city of Athens and it is a temple that has been built in the honour of Poseidon, the god of seas. It belongs to the 5th century BC and references confirm only 6 columns that still stand, however the place is marvellous. It is mostly visited at the evening when the sun sets and starts to sink in the sea and reflects a golden hue to the remaining part of the day. This is one place you can freely roam around as you envisage early sailors having offered offerings to Poseidon before setting of for the seas. And if you are very adventurous you can go swimming at one of the nearby beaches before proceeding back to Athens.

Epidaurus

If one wants to delve in ancient theatre or appreciate beautiful sceneries than Epidaurus is worth a visit. This ancient city developed as a city of health; the site contained the Sanctuary of Asclepius, the Greek god of medicine. Citizens of the Greek world used to come here in order to get a treatment for various illnesses. Yet, the drawings of the show-stealing ancient theatre of Epidaurus are still a wonder of today's applications. Dating back to the 4th century BC this is one of the oldest theatres that impressed by its acoustics: if you stand in the middle of the stage and whisper, you will be heard at the top of the slope. That is something which leaves one wondering at the genius of ancient Greek engineers when you sit in the theatre envisaging the drama that must have unfolded in the arena.

Ancient Athens agora

When you are strolling through the Ancient Agora of Athens there is nothing that tells you are treading on the same ground Socrates, Plato and other Greek philosophers supported on. This used to be the center of Athenian city and it was here that the citizens used to congregate and engage in politics, philosophy and other matters of their daily existence. Other features that should have been and probably are in Agora include public buildings, markets and temples the most outstanding among them being the Temple of Hephaestus which has been preserved in the present day. The plaza is now an archaeological park and it's rather quiet; good for a walk as you absorb history. The Stoa of Attalos which is located next to the site was reconstructed in 1950s and contains a museum to explain more about daily life in Athens.

Rhodes Old Town

Rhodes is a historical island and there is no better representation of this than the old town of the island. This medieval city is one of the most developed in the regions so despite the walls and gates it is one of the best preserved cities in Europe. The Knights of St. John were especially active in the 14th and in the 15th centuries and they are responsible for the construction of most of what you can see today. Exploring the site of narrow cobbled streets in the Old Town, and the atmosphere makes one feel he or she is living in the Stone Age. Among those, you will be able to see such attractions as the Palace of the Grand Master, the Street of the Knights, and many other medieval sights. But the ideas have not ended in medieval ages only, Rhodes also shares its connection with the ancient world. Here in Rhodes once stood the Colossus that one of the seven wonders of the Ancient World, however nothing remains today.

Seven of these monasteries are grouped together on the peninsula of Mount Athos called the "Athonite State."

Mount Athos is the most outstanding historical religious site of Greece. This region at Northern Greece is occupying lands of modern monasteries for more than thousand years, here are locating 20 monasteries. There is no doubt that what adds a unique zest to Mount Athos is that it does not only function as an Independent Monastery but possesses a highly independent status legally. Men are the only ones who are permitted to go to the island and again, entry here is very limited with only a few permits to visit issued in a day.

Nevertheless, if you cannot come there, it is interesting to know the stories and history of Mount Athos. The monasteries harbor some of the most valuable religious icons, manuscripts, and relics, and therefore is one of the most religious regions in the globe.

What is Greece Famous for?

Greece is a country that is very dear to people inasmuch it is dear to me. Just like the majority of you, if I hear Greece, the first thing that comes into my mind is those seemingly picture perfect islands with pretty white houses and the most beautiful deep blue sea. But oh my God, Greece is so much more than picturesque view (although it offers some of the most stunning sceneries I have ever come across). Alright, without further ado let's explore the key aspect that makes Greece truly shine on the international level.

Ancient History and Mythology

First and foremost, Greece is the country of myths and legends, as well as the history of more than thousands of years. It is the home of western civilization and it has shaped so much of the culture that we have today. Consider it as the birthplace of democracy, Philosophy, theatre and some of the significant concepts in science and arts.

From the great columns of the Parthenon in Athens to the ruins of the Temple of Apollo in Delphi there is archaeology history that is still alive. If you are planning to take a walk around any big city or an administrative town, do not be surprised to come across at least two archaeological sites. The whole ambiance of the place gives one a feel of going back to history when you are in the middle of ruins that date back 2,200 years. But let's not forget about Greek myths, which involve gods and goddesses, heroes and heroines and astonishing stories. Myths say that Zeus, Athena and Hercules have once ruled and although they are real figures and not just fictional characters, they are still embedded in the contemporary Greek society.

Stunning Islands and Beaches

If there's one thing which almost everyone would associate with Greece then it has to be the islands. There are more than 6000 islands in total however only 200 of them are populated which makes it even more appealing for those who are fans of traveling. While it is easy to get captivated with the beautiful sunsets, blue-domed churches, and volcanic sandy beaches of Santorini. Still, there are other Greek destinations for tourists and has its own charm such as Mykonos, Crete, Rhodes, and Naxos.

Every single island is very unique and this has made them have their own personalities. For example, Mykonos is for you if you want more luxurious beach bar and shinning night clubs. , meanwhile is rich in history having been the home to the ancient Minoan civilization which housed the magnificent Palace of Knossos. There is, for instance, the picturesque beauty of the typical Greek islands such as Paros or Milos: enjoying the sea and the sun during the day and having a delicious fish meal at an appropriately rustic tavern at night.

Talking of beaches, Greece has some of the best beaches in the world. Think of endless sandy beaches, small bays and what seems to be every colour of the sea. Some beaches are busy and developed; one can go for water sports or lie down on the sand and drink beers. Some are secluded and quite isolated and maybe you don't get to see another person for many miles. That is the beauty of Greece; is you can get any type of beach your heart desires.

Delicious Food and Drink

Well, let's speak of food – because, indeed, Greece is a country of food enthusiasts. The Mediterranean diet is famous for its health benefits as well as delicious meals, and, as it will be seen in Greece, tasty as well. This has it all, fresh food, local and if you are a fan of flavors you are in for a treat.

Greece is also renowned for its wine excellently produced red and white through the vineyards. The Ancient Greeks who were on the region today known as Santorini had been has been cultivating grapes for wine productions for several centuries. Of course, you don't leave the country without tasting ouzo, the alcoholic beverage that incorporates anise as its leading ingredient. It is perhaps more satisfying to drink it slowly, along with the ambient chatter and some yummy appetizers, or meze.

Hospitality (Philoxenia)

A welcoming and friendly disposition of citizens is felt in Greece like few other places in the globe. There's even a word for it: The Greeks have a word for hospitable disposition which is Philoxenia or love of strangers, this tradition is well rooted in their culture, and from the time one sets foot in Greece, it feels like they are at home. From the last place I stayed in a surprisingly friendly family guest house on a remote small island to the city restaurants the locals will be more than friendly. I might get a free glass of the wine or some piece of a sweet, and people are quite willing of sharing their stories and the stories of Greece.

This generosity and friendliness are not just directed towards the foreigners as can be observed from the following examples. It is so much a norm in Greece that it practically has become a way of life in the country. You'll meet it when people are getting out of their homes, when people are sitting down for their meals, and when and where people are dancing around a fire or baking cakes.

It is one of the feelings that makes this country feel like home even if it is the first time to make a visit to this country.

Spectacular Sunsets

Sunsets in Greece are exceptionally beautiful with the most famous one in the island of santorini. Seeing the sun sets behind the buildings and getting golden hue with stunning white colored buildings and sea is an amazing experience. But, as it is clearly seen, Santorini is not the only destination where people can observe an incredible sunset. Sceneries are present throughout the country and they range from steep hills of Athens to the beautiful beaches of Crete and the beautiful cliffs of Meteora.

This and much more remains appealing, be it you are on a beach chair, or at a beach bar enjoying a cocktail, or on top of some Ancient ruin, there is something spectacular seeing the Greek sky turn pink, orange and purple at sunset.

Vibrant Festivals and Traditions

One of the things that Greeks find very important is celebration, and there are festivals and events throughout the year that will let you a sneak preview on what Greeks are all about. The most popular of them is Easter which is regarded as the major celebration in Greece. It is a season which is characterized by the coming together of families and also by lighting candles especially at night to symbolize the resurrection of Christ. The Easter in Greece is an ideal time of the year to experience the singing in the church, the dancing in the streets, and not to mention the food wherein it is traditionally the season for lambs.

There is also Carnival though it is mainly enjoyed in the town of Patras which usually has the largest Carnival festival in the entire country. It is all carnival like with dancing, music, parades, and anything else that could fit into the play.

Most of the islands also have their local fairs which are usually held in honor of a particular saint or some other religious personality. These are identified as panigiria and these will offer a one-stop platform to immerse in the local dances, music, and food and interact with the locals. It is one of a kind, exuberant and this vibe is in the audience.

Dramatic Landscapes

Greece is not only a country of beautiful beaches and island but it is also characterized by large geographic features. The country is very rich with mountains, gorges and cliffs to enable the hikers achieve their dreams of adventure. Olympus, the mountain that was believed to be the dwelling place of Gods is the tallest mountain in Greece and is one of the most climbed mountains in the country. If you are not keen into climbing its peaks, the whole place is surrounded by a National Park and there are numerous breathtaking places and wildlife to explore.

There is Meteora, which is as bizarre as it can be by having huge rocks on which monasteries are placed. It in itself is a UNESCO World heritage site and is a place that seems that it has dropped right out of a fairy tale. It is possible to climb the monasteries some of which are inhabited even now; you can enjoy the quietude and the magnificent views of the valleys.

Art, Music, and Dance

Greek people have been involved in art for perhaps thousands of years and that is still the case today. Most of the sites in the country are packed with galleries, museums, and other cultural attractions of whatever type of art you may be interested in; from pottery to painting, sculptures, etc. Greece also has quite a diverse music tradition and its musical instruments such as bouzouki, a type of stringed instrument and the more recently, styles of music including rebetiko- a type of folk music from the urban areas is very popular to date. If you can, attend to live band in a local tavern, or better yet a concert in one of the old theaters of Greece.

And as you can see dancing is also an essential part of our lives. Sirtaki known today also as "Zorba dance" from the movie Zorba the Greek is among the most popular Greek dances. One will chance to watch it during festivals and celebrations, the dancers join their hands and dance to the Greek music. What makes them special is the ability to entice many people to join in, could be because you see people jumping in.

Chapter Two

Top Attractions to Visit in Greece

Every traveler would love to visit Greece and it is not very hard to comprehend why. From the Roman times archaeological sites and cities teeming with life, through bright islands which seem to be created especially for sun lovers and ending on mountainous villages which are perfect for calm tourists. So depending on the kind of traveler you are— if you're a history enthusiast, or just a beach lover, or a great food lover or just someone who loves the sceneries, then you'll find yourself losing yourself in Greece. So let's go through some of the wonderful tourist sites in Greece the traveler shouldn't miss.

Athens - The Historic Soul of Greece

We have to begin with Athens because, you know… it's the birthplace of the entire Greek narrative. It is not only the core of contemporary Greek presence but also a city where the past of ancient people seems living in each stone. The New Acropolis which is located at the summit of the city also deserves mention. Walk about the ruins, and it is almost impossible not feel amazed at the ancestors of man. Among the places, one must mention the Parthenon dedicated to the goddess Athena, the Erechtheion and the Temple of Athena Nike that is currently in ruins but still inspiring with its view.

You'll never run out of things to do here but when the sun gets tiresome and the ways in, head down to Plaka, the old town below the Acropolis. Here is something which includes thin streets and small roads with beautiful houses and small taverns or shops with handmade products. The blend of both old and young is well seen in Athens and that is why it is full of character. Contemporary art museums alongside upbeat wine and beer establishments and food trucks give a lively taste to this historic city.

Santorini – For You the Perfect Sunsets

Whenever people see pictures of Greece more often than not they are actually seeing pictures of Santorini. You will find this picture-perfect island in the Aegean Sea, with the enchanting white and blue buildings perched on the cliffs with the sea below. The sunsets which are witnessed here are simply legends which one would hear of. Besides, the spectacle of the sun setting and getting merged with the water followed by the rays of light reflecting on the island's villages is something to marvel at.

But that's where it ends to beautify – The Greek island of Santorini has more to offer than just the physical beauty. Not that one can simply sit and gaze at the view, which might be satisfying for some (and should be for a couple of hours at least!). Fira and Oia are two main towns of the island where one can take a relaxed walk as the town boasts of numerous cafés, art galleries, and boutiques. The island of Akrotiri which is one of the most famous attractions to visit is a Minoan settlement that was covered under thick layers of volcanic ash approximately 3600 years ago thus attracting be likened to the modern day Pompeii. For sunbathing, there has to do beautiful sandy beaches which are rarely seen, there are black, white and red sands because of the volcanic nature of Santorini.

A World of Its Own Case Study – Crete

Being the largest of the Greek islands, travelling to Crete makes you feel that you have moved to a different world altogether. It is one of the countries of the world that is bordered by some of the most beautiful rugged mountains, sandy coastlines, archaeological sites, and bountiful cities. The capital city of the island is Heraklion where one of the greatest vacationer attractions of the state lies, the Palace of Knossos; the dwelling place of the famed Minoan civilization. Roam around inside the complex of ruins with your mind attempting to unveil the myths of the Minotaur that came from its ground.

However, what's really important to know is that Crete is not only history. The geophysical features include gorges of which the longest Gorge in Europe is the Samaria Gorge. Travelling through this natural landmark is one of the fascinating experiences that one would not hesitate to undertake. For sightseeing, visit theimple tourist place of Chania's Venetian Harbour & if you are tired then go to the beautiful beach of Elafonissi Beach which has pink sand & crystal water. A great experience is also the Cretan villages themselves which offer visitors raki (the home-made Greek spirit) and some of the best meat – based Cretan cuisine: lamb, fresh cheeses and sweets glazed with honey.

Mykonos - The Island of Life Entertainments

Mykonos is possibly the image Greece takes out for a swim during summer; it is the epitome of trendiness. Being synonymous to TNT parties by the beach and dancing all night till the sun comes up in the sky, Mykonos provides all that you desire. However, as you will soon find out, there is much more to this island than gets to meet eyes in the clubs, bars and discos at nights.

In the daytime, visit Mykonos Chora which is a beautiful town where buildings are constructed in white and blue, full of local café and international luxurious brands. Do not forget to visit the windmills which are among the famous symbols of the island. If you want to have a really quiet time, one can go to the Archaeological Museum in Mykonos or even just cross the sea about fifteen minutes to Delos, which is another significant archaeological site in Greece. Delos was once one of the centers of the greek world, and moving around the ruins, one will feel like he is back to the ancient greek epoch.

Of course if you are here for the sand and the sea then I don't think you will be disappointed at all. While **Paradise Beach and Super Paradise Beach** are the places for celebration with music and dancing in addition to sunning. If you as for something less active, **Agios Sostis** is a very beautiful and less crowded place.

Meteora – Monasteries IN THE SKY

If you dream of coming to a place, which seemed to come out of a fairy-tale or science fiction movie, Meteora will definitely meet your expectations.

The enormous rocks of Meteora host centuries old monasteries on top of them, thus making it one of the most stunning places in Greece. Some of the monasteries resemble tremendous fortresses hanging from the sky, so the name 'Meteora' translates as 'suspended in the air' for a reason.

The monasteries are of 14th century and many of them exist to the present day. To get to them, one has to get to the steep stone steps hewn on the rock and to get to them is more than a worth. There are stunning wall paintings, exceptional documents, and tranquillity that can't be described.

And if you're not into history at all, still, Meteora is a definite must-see for the beautiful surrounding it has. The panorama from above is truly astonishing: the surrounding cliffs go down to valleys at certain distance and there are mountains in the vicinity. It's like a piece of fairy tale right in the middle of the country, and therefore the area has been given the UNESCO World Heritage status.

Rhodes – A Blend of Ancient and the Medieval

Rhodes is arguably one of the most intriguing islands of Greece due to the fact that it boasts both of ancient and medieval attraction sites. Old Town of Rhodes: the island's star attraction and a UNESCO site; it looks like it has been lifted right out of a medieval fairytale. Somer sedate houses are laid out along the picturesque stone-paved roads, and, following its curves, one comes to the Palace of the Grand Master of the Orders of the Knights of St John which were founded during the Crusades. The walls, gates and towers have retained their ancient look and this castle offers one of the best examples of the medieval architecture in Europe.

Outside the Old Town there are certainly plenty of things to do and see in Rhodes. The old city of Lindos, built on a hill on the seashore, is without doubts one of the most beautiful views and provides the visitors with the feeling of ancient Greece. As for the beach, there are pretty Anthony Quinn Bay and Tsambika Beach only within the island's territory.

Rhodes is also famous for its hospitality and relaxed tempo of residents' lives. Foot is the best to get around and stroll through the historical neighborhoods with the occasional sip of coffee or eating and souvlaki.

Nafplio: Soft, Pink and Affection

If you want some romance and art mixed up in history, follow the directions and go to Nafplio. Nafplio is a small seaside town in the Peloponnese Peninsula which was the first capital of modern Greece and there is something about it that will make you fall in love with the place. The Palamidi Fortress is the most recognizable structure and if you are fit, you can actually take the 970 steps stairs to reach the top. It is so worth the while to trek up the town and this side of the sea.

Nafplio is the kind of place where you don't necessarily need a plan of what to do in your day because you can just wake up, walk the cobblestone streets or stop for a coffee by the harbor. The Bourtzi Castle, situated at a small island nearby the coast is also beautiful and must visit place. There is always the chance to grab a gondola and head out to this Venetian constructed fortress while feeling the sea breeze.

Thessaloniki – the place of Culture and Tastes

While being the second largest city of Greece, Thessaloniki seems to play second fiddle to Athens but it certainly has a personality of its own and much to offer. Being one of the youngest cities in Greece with a rich cultural background and great food heritage, Thessaloniki is a place that never cease to amaze its visitors.

Most visitors are familiar with Great White Tower which is the elementary concern of the city and from the top of this one can have the best view of the city and the seas. Thessaloniki is also home to some of the best Byzantine architecture in Greece, including the Church of Agios Dimitrios and the Rotunda, both UNESCO World Heritage sites.

Food is a huge part of life in Thessaloniki, and you'll find some of the best street food in Greece here. Try a bougatsa, a flaky pastry filled with either sweet cream or savory cheese, or grab a gyro from one of the many stalls around the city. The nightlife here is lively too, with plenty of bars, live music venues, and cafés where you can soak up the city's creative spirit

1. Athens
Sights to See:

- **The Acropolis and Parthenon:** The heart of ancient Athens with its iconic temples.
- **Acropolis Museum:** Showcases artifacts from the Acropolis.
- **Plaka Neighborhood:** A charming area with winding streets and neoclassical architecture.

Activities:

- Take a guided tour of the Acropolis.
- Stroll through Plaka and shop for souvenirs.
- Enjoy Greek food at a taverna.

Address: The Acropolis of Athens, Athens 105 58, Greece
Opening Hours: Daily from 8:00 AM – 8:00 PM (varies seasonally)
Ticket Price:

- €20 (April 1st to October 31st)
- €10 (November 1st to March 31st)
- Combination tickets for various archaeological sites: €30

2. Santorini
Sights to See:

- **Oia Village:** Famous for its blue-domed churches and sunset views.
- **Akrotiri Archaeological Site:** Minoan ruins buried by a volcanic eruption.
- **Fira Town:** The Island's bustling capital with cafés and shops.

Activities:

- Watch the sunset in Oia.
- Visit the wineries of Santorini for a wine-tasting experience.
- Explore the black-sand beaches of Kamari or Perissa.

Address: Oia, Santorini 847 02, Greece

Opening Hours: Akrotiri Site: Daily from 8:00 AM – 8:00 PM

Ticket Price:

- Akrotiri Archaeological Site: €12
- Combined ticket (Akrotiri, Ancient Thera, and Museum of Prehistoric Thera): €15

3. Crete
Sights to See:

- **Palace of Knossos:** The largest Bronze Age archaeological site on Crete.

- **Samaria Gorge:** One of Europe's longest gorges.

- **Heraklion Archaeological Museum:** One of the top museums in Greece, showcasing Minoan artifacts.

Activities:

- Hike through Samaria Gorge (16 km) and explore the natural beauty of Crete.
- Visit Elafonissi Beach with its pink sands.
- Taste traditional Cretan dishes like dakos and grilled lamb.

Address: Knossos Palace, Knossos 714 09, Crete, Greece

Opening Hours:

- **Knossos Palace:** Daily from 8:00 AM – 8:00 PM
- **Samaria Gorge:** Open from May to October (closed in winter due to weather conditions)

Ticket Price:

- Knossos Palace: €15
- Samaria Gorge: €5

4. Mykonos
Sights to See:

- **Mykonos Windmills:** Iconic windmills overlooking the town.
- **Delos Island:** An archaeological site considered the birthplace of Apollo.
- **Little Venice:** A picturesque area with waterfront bars and restaurants.

Activities:

- Enjoy the lively nightlife at beach clubs like Paradise Beach.

- Take a boat trip to Delos Island and explore the ruins.
- Wander through the narrow streets of Mykonos Town (Chora).

Address: Mykonos Town, Mykonos 846 00, Greece

Opening Hours:

- **Delos Island:** Open from 8:00 AM – 3:00 PM (closed on Mondays)
- **Ticket Price:**
- **Delos Island: €12 (standard ticket)**
- Free entry to the windmills area

5. Meteora

Sights to See:

- **Monasteries of Meteora:** Six active monasteries perched on top of towering rock formations.
- **Theopetra Cave:** A prehistoric archaeological site nearby.

Activities:

- Visit the monasteries (you'll need to climb stairs, so bring good shoes).
- Take a guided hiking tour to explore the natural landscape.
- Watch the sunset over the cliffs for an unforgettable experience.

Address: Meteora, Kalabaka 422 00, Greece

Opening Hours:

- Varies by monastery, but most are open between 9:00 AM – 5:00 PM
- Closed on some religious holidays (check in advance)

Ticket Price:
- Entrance to each monastery: €3 per person
- Combined hiking and monastery tours: Prices start from €30

6. Rhodes

Sights to See:
- **Palace of the Grand Master:** A medieval fortress in the Old Town.
- **Acropolis of Lindos:** A cliff-top archaeological site with views of the sea.
- **Anthony Quinn Bay:** A beautiful beach named after the actor who starred in The Guns of Navarone.

Activities:
- Explore the cobbled streets of Rhodes Old Town.
- Relax on the beaches like Tsambika Beach and Faliraki Beach.
- Visit the Valley of the Butterflies during summer.

Address: Palace of the Grand Master, Ippoton, Rhodes 851 00, Greece

Opening Hours:
- Palace of the Grand Master: Daily from 8:00 AM – 8:00 PM
- Acropolis of Lindos: Daily from 8:00 AM – 7:30 PM

Ticket Price:

- Palace of the Grand Master: €6
- Acropolis of Lindos: €12

7. Nafplio
Sights to See:

- **Palamidi Fortress:** A Venetian fortress with nearly 1,000 steps to the top.
- **Bourtzi Castle:** A small fortress on an island in the harbor.
- **Arvanitia Beach:** A small, pebbly beach near the town.

Activities:

- Climb up to the Palamidi Fortress for panoramic views.
- Take a boat ride to Bourtzi Castle.
- Enjoy a romantic evening walk along the waterfront promenade.

- **Address:** Palamidi Fortress, Nafplio 211 00, Greece

Opening Hours:

- Palamidi Fortress: Daily from 8:00 AM – 7:30 PM

Ticket Price:

- Palamidi Fortress: €8
- Bourtzi Castle: €4 (includes boat trip)

8. Thessaloniki
Sights to See:

- **White Tower:** A symbol of the city and a museum showcasing Thessaloniki's history.
- **Archaeological Museum of Thessaloniki:** Home to artifacts from ancient Macedonia.
- **Church of Agios Dimitrios:** A UNESCO-listed Byzantine church dedicated to the city's patron saint.

Activities:
- Walk along the seaside promenade and enjoy the cafés and views.
- Visit the Rotunda, another UNESCO site and one of the oldest buildings in the city.
- Dive into the vibrant street food scene—don't miss the bougatsa pastries.

- **Address:** White Tower, Thessaloniki 546 21, Greece

Opening Hours:
- White Tower: Daily from 8:00 AM – 8:00 PM

Ticket Price:
- White Tower: €4
- Archaeological Museum: €8

Chapter Three
What to Do in Greece

When the word Greece is mentioned for most people, the first images that come to their mind are old structures, beautiful sand beaches and houses built on the cliffs, usually white and facing the sea. Yes, Greece is all of that mentioned above; however, it is much, much more than what has been described. If history, adventures, delicious food or just nice tan in Mediterranean climate is your cup of tea, there is no shortage of interesting sites to see in this country. Without any further delay let's take a look and see what you are able to do in Greece.

Explore Ancient History

Every corner of Greece opens a new window to history that's as old as the country itself, literally. Especially for history lovers, or even if you wouldn't call yourself a history lover, there is no chance you would not see some of the historical sites during the Greek island tour.

Begin in Athens, of course, where the **Parthenon** looms over the city. When approaching Parthenon one of the greatest and most recognizable works of art of ancient Greece, one cannot but amaze. Don't miss the museum either – its collection of various exhibits are mouthwatering and gives you the feeling that you are getting to know this legendary place.

I wanted to say that, if you happen to visit Delpho, you will get a chance to know the enigmatic part of Ancient Greece. This place was once regarded as the primordial heart of the earth which visitors flocked to as to the Oracle of Apollo. Try to picture yourself being at the Temple of Apollo with lochs at the backdrop, and you will know why such place was considered holy.

There are many tourist attractions in Crete, most famous of them is the **Palace of Knossos**, where the Minoan civilization existed and the place which is associated with the Minotaur. There is a fact that this stock is very old and its existence is still shrouded with a veil of mystery – one can spend here several hours exploring its corridors.

Relax on Stunning Beaches

The beaches of Greece are among the most admired ones in the globe for a number of good reasons. It has clean waters, powdery sand, and most importantly excellent scenery thus making Greece among the best coastal destinations in the world. There are just a shameful number of various beaches to select from with or without a vivid nightlife.

Santorini is most likely among the Seven Wonders of the World and so are its beaches which are as breathtaking as the views here. Red Beach is named simply because it is actually a beach with red sand, cliffs and clear blue sea put together in lovely contrast. Or visit the Kamari Beach to feel the sand which is black volcanic sand. In fact, it's worth mentioning that the beaches in Santorini are not only suitable for sunbathing and swimming but are more ideal of capturing views of the islands surroundings.

For those more tropical, beach-type views, **Mykonos** has got you sorted. This is where you can spend your days lying on the soft sand of Paradise Beach or dancing and sipping cocktails to music all night at Super Paradise Beach. However, if you are in search of a calmer place for relaxing by a sea and not jamming along with people, there is Agios Sostis.

That island paradise **Elafonisi**, if you already find yourself in Crete, should not be missed. Its pink sands and shallow turquoise water make it look like what you might see in a dreamland. It is especially considered for families as the water does not we reach deep for a long distance, so children can play in it.

Island Hopping Adventures

That being said the Greek islands are not limited to just Santorini and Mykonos and there is definitely more than just beautiful beaches that you can have there if that is all they'll be expecting. More than 200 of those are populated and each of them boasts its unique identity, traditions and scenic views. One cannot beat the beauty of island hopping, especially when touring beautiful Greece which is so diverse.

Discover the charm of Naxos; enjoy sandy shores of the largest island in the Cyclades, wander around the lovely mountainous villages and visit the archaeological sites. This place is less flashy compared to the previous ones and is well set for scooters rental to roam around at your own pace.

Here, on **Paros island**, you will get to enjoy the best combination of relaxation and action. The traditional villages, such as Naoussa and Lefkes, are a real joy to explore, while the beaches, such as **Kolymbithres**, are the perfect place for a leisurely swim. Everybody who is passionate about water activities can consider Paros one of the best beaches for windsurfing and kiting in Greece.

And, as an unconventional out of the way sort of place, it's definitely special: Milos it is. Actually, the island of Milos offers some of the most exotic beach experiences in the entire Mediterranean, let alone Greece: smooth, white volcanic rock of Sarakiniko Beach, for example. Visit sea grottos, sunbathe on beaches that are not reachable by car or walk through the island's rocky cliffs for quite the view.

Indulge in Greek Food

Food is one of the important factors which makes your tour to Greece a most enjoyable one. It can be said that Greek food is definitely one of the unadulterated forms of cooking which uses highly fresh and locally available food items to create dishes which would evoke a dancing movement on your tongue.

Try the first course of **meze**, the Greek equivalent of Spanish tapas. Meze are small dishes meant for sharing; favorites are **tzatziki (yogurt and cucumber with garlic), saganaki (cheese fried), dolmades (stuffed grape vine leaves)**. Accompany them with a glass of ouzo – anise flavoured aperitif which is a Greek speciality – and you've started as you mean to go on.

The must is seafood if you are on an island. If you have some more time on your hands you should definitely taste our famous grilled octopus or fish and calamari just caught from the sea while sitting by the sea and experiencing the real Mediterranean Sea breeze. Before you leave the table, it is customary to have a taste of baklava, a honey and nut sweet pastry or loukoumades which are honeyed doughnuts.

Discover Greece's Nature Trails

Yes, Greece is not a country which is only about sea, sand, and history; it has some of the most beautiful terrains too. Hiking and outdoor activities are endless if you fancy yourself a long nature walk or a rugged trail experience.

The other great place for hiking in Greece is **Mount Olympus**, the mountain of the gods according to mythology. Trekkking to the top of Olympus is a stunning but a bit hard activity. Even if the area doesn't get you to the top, the rim of the national park is filled with gorgeous trails that provide stunning views and opportunities to view the regions exotic plant and animal life.

In Crete, for example, the **Samaria Gorge** is one of the most beautiful gorges to hike through in the longest gorge system in Europe. The path leads you along steep cliffs, by historic remains, near a flowing river and culminates at the Libyan sea. It takes at least a day full day to enjoy it fully but none the less it's one exciting adventure.

This one is more easy going however it should not be missed, Meteora. Opted with monasteries here today standing on these giant rocks although many of the above structures are still functional. When hiking the trails of Meteora, one is privileged to see these (what looks like) 'flying' monasteries and the beauteous countryside around them. The air is serene and theological, which should make for good reading and sunbathing, and people actually look content here. The recommendation made to the guest is to take a cruise around the Aegean.

Most of the cruises originating from Athens or Piraeus go on to explore the better known islands of Santorini, Mykonos, Rhodes, and Crete. During the day, there are some amazing stops that allow you to tour each island's attractions including walking around archaeological sites, sunbathing and swimming, shopping or having a traditional Greek meal at a coastal restaurant a.k.a taverna.

For something more personal, you can also sail on **sailboat or catamaran**, and create your own schedule. Imagine rowing without a precise path towards secluded bays, deserted islands, and sandy shores and anchor whenever you want. This is your classic Greek island experience if you have been watching movies like Zorba the Greek or visited Greece often.

Enjoy Greek Nightlife

Regardless, the Greeks most certainly do know how to have a good time, and nightlife in Greece is as diverse as the country is diverse. Particularly if dancing to a popular tune is your thing, then Mykonos is absolutely the nightlife king of Greece. While some beach clubs mix music into the daytime scene to keep things going through the night, after sundown, there are plenty of nightclubs where TOP DJs from around the world are performing.

Thus, nightlife in Athens is as vibrant but more various than in Mykonos. From rooftop bars with Athens' stretching views to taverns where you can savor Greeks music, almost everything is available to explore in Athens. For something slightly different, why not sample the local bouzoukia clubs, where it is possible to watch groups of traditional musicians and singers performing and even be encouraged to dance.

That is a really important thing to know because on the islands people are not as tense as they are in continent. In places like Paros, Naxos, and Milos most of the night entertaining kind of happens in beach bars, seafood eating joints and taverns. Take a drink, sit by the sea and relax and watch the sun setting in the Mediterranean as you gaze up smiling feeling the comforting heat of a warm summer night in Greece.

Discover more about the Culture and traditions of Greece

This is actually one of the greatest strengths of Greece: its cultural history is not only long and storied, but vibrant to this day. Food, dance, religion, music, history, drama, architecture...The list is quite extensive when it comes to experiencing the Culture of Greece.

If you are here in the spring then you are in for a treat because Greek Easter is one of the biggest events in Greece. The celebrations include candlelight procession, church services, food sharing and firework display. This is a happy time for families to be together, and as a guest you will find that you are enthusiastically welcomed throughout the year

Panigiria are also represented in the whole year as villagers celebrate Greek traditional feasts in villages and some islands in Greece. These are usually celebrations of a local saint, with much music, dance, and a lot of that old favorite, all kinds of food. The Panigiri of Agios Panteleimonas on Naxos is one of the most famous ones and you can dance to recorded music late into the night. It only seems natural that you might be invited to eat the traditional roasted lamb or to take a sip of raki the strong local spirit.

One can also watch a play at one of the many theatres that dotted the Greek landscape, many of which are used till this date. **The Epidaurus Theatre**, probably one of the most well preserved ancient theatres, stages performances of ancient Greek drama during the Athens and Epidaurus Festival which takes place in summer. Something happens when you watch a tragedy or a comedy enacted right where those plays were scripted thousands of years ago.

For more information on traditional Greek crafts almost every island and village hosts crafts makers who inherited the tradition. Thus in Crete traditional crafts can be seen with the artisans at work in pottery & weaving; the town of Lindos in Rhodes is born for ceramic art.

Go Wine Tasting

The Greeks have been producing wine for over 4500 years, and winemaking in the country is still going strong. For the wine enthusiast or for the casual consumer who extends his palate to the occasional glass of grape juice, a visit to vinery in any Greek island is certainly an edible treasure.

This volcano is the reason for the Grey which makes the wine grown in the island of Santorini some of the rarest in the world. The wine of the island, **Assyrtiko**, has a fresh and nicely sharp note and should be drunk especially with fish. Wine factories in the island provide guests with tours followed by wine tasting in which guest get to taste great wines while overlooking the caldera.

On the mainland, Nemea, a region in the Peloponnese produces particularly succulent red wines labelled Agiorgitiko. The town of Nemea has some lovely wine producers where wine tasting tours are offered as well as the ability to tour the vineyards as well as participate in the grape picking if you come in the autumn.

Crete is also great for wine lovers; they boast their own varieties, Vidiano and Liatiko wines are now famous internationally. There are wine roads on the island where you can travel around the countryside learning about and tasting the lovely Cretan wine while enjoying local cheese and olives.

Dive into Adventure
Ideally, if you are an adventure lover and enjoy in outdoor activities, Greece is a great country to visit. Some of the major activities that are closely associated with this zone include water activities such as swimming, water rafting, and mountain hiking, among others.

If water sports are your game, then boarding and sailing is huge in Greece with main destinations on paros, naxos and kos. The Meltemi winds that rise in the Aegean Sea makes these islands ideal to catch the wind and thrive on the waves. Usually, if you have never visited the archery range before, there is no reason to worry because there is a number of schools which teach archery to complete novices.

The two are also ideal for Greece; scuba diving and snorkeling. Among the seas that are full of fish, the Aegean and Ionians seas seem to be the most popular among divers as well as waters around the islands of Zakynthos, Corfu and Crete. Swim beneath the surface and you may be surrounded by turtles and fish, if you're lucky, even a wrecked ship.

But if you don't wish to go for a water adventure here is what you can do: **hiking and mountain biking**. Caution is needed when cycling or walking since the Cyclades islands are hilly and have fantastic views of the sea. Here on Crete you can take the E4 European Walking Path which crosses the island and which has some of the most beautiful views.

If you want to get your pulse racing you could always try your hand at some rock climbing as **Kalymnos** is one of the best places in the world to do so. Climbing routes numbering in the hundreds, beautiful sea views, excellent weather conditions... Kalymnos climbing is something many climbers simply cannot turn their backs on.

Shop like a Local
Shopping in Greece is fun whether for luxury brands, arts and crafts, or any other novelty gifts. There are some fine shopping targets in Athens like, Ermou Street for international brands and Monastiraki for more

ethnic feel shopping. One finds literally everything here, from antiques to jewelries, leather products and many others and it is Located in Monastiraki. Who told you that you can never find anything?

And on the islands there are opportunities to buy up unique products that will be a fitting gift or a memorandum. My recommendation is not to go to Santorini without tasting the volcanic wine or, perhaps, taking a jar of fava beans, which are native to the island. If you have been to Crete you should know that you can take high quality olive oil, honey and handmade pottery products with you.

Chora is the heartbeat of Mykonos where you'll find an array of boutiques selling beautiful clothing's, art and jewelries amongst others. And if you're in Rhodes, do not fail to visit the shops selling refurbished pottery, leather works and embroidered fabrics crafted by the locals.

Enjoy a Spa Day

Thus after going through all the sightseeing and adventures occasionally, one feels the need to wind up a little. Fortunately, there is a list of exclusive spas and thermal springs in Greece where you can reverse the process.

One of the most popular islands is **Evia** with thermal baths situated in town called **Edipsos** famous for its curative water since antiquity. It is recommended that people travel to **Egoreal** to take in the hot springs because they heal everything from arthritis to skin diseases. Today, there are a few spas in the area where you can enjoy services offered by a masseuse, spa, such as a bath in mud or water, massage, and hydrotherapy. If you are lucky enough to be visiting Santorini, you might want to spend a day pampered in one of the island's fine spa hotels. Some provide treatments that resemble beauty products commonly found in their area such as a volcanic mud and wine bath. It also possible to do a private sun set boat ride and get down to the island for a natural hot spring water bath in natural mineral water.

In the mainland one of the most popular resort is **Loutraki** near Athens which boasts of its hydro therapy centres and therapeutic springs. This is especially true when you take a day to visit one of the spas here, thermal baths and aromatherapy and other treatments available while you take in the beauty of the countryside reminiscent of Greece.

Major Outdoors Activities you can explore in Greece

The idea that Greece is just ruins and sand is one of the biggest misconceptions about this wonderful country it's outdoors adventure zone.

No matter if you feel like a thrilling trekking, a silent kayaking along the sea shore, or something in between you can find it in Greece. The geography here is as varied as the region's history; mountains, gorges, forests and vast coastal plains can be found here. Therefore as I mentioned if you are an outdoor kind of person then this is good news for you. Now let's look at several of the greatest things you can do on the outdoors in Greece.

Hiking and Trekking

Greece is a hiker's paradise. To look at the rocky terrains, and quiet beaches with scenic beauty and small elevation, and those who wish to take relatively intense treks, there is no dearth of it here. Undoubtedly, one of the most popular hikes you can complete is the **Mount Olympus**, named after the gods' residence. Standing at a height of **2,917 meters (9,570 feet)** it is Greece's tallest mountain and the climb to the summit is as appealing as the views from the top. But if climbing is not your thing, there are other trails that range in distance from around the mountain and give the same feeling of adventure and beauty.

For something much more laid back but just as stunning, the Samaria Gorge in Crete is the place to go. This is one of Europe's longest gorge stretching 16 kilometers, 10 miles and hiking through the gorge makes me feel like I have entered a different world. This hiking trail is a visual delight because it features towering cliffs, crystal clear rivers and ancient ruins.

This part of the walk is completed at a picturesque seaside village of **Agia roumeli** where one can take a cool dip in the Libyan sea. It is an all-day affair that you are not like to forget in hurry.

If you are there, Cyclades has hundreds of trails awaiting hikers and long picturesque vistas over the turquoise waters of the Aegean Sea. There is an outstanding trail on Naxos, through the old villages with the finds of archaeological interest, and the more famous Santorini, where the trail from Fira to Oia cross the cliffs presenting you the incredible panoramic view of the Caldera.

Sailing and Island Hopping

Greece, with its 6,000 plus islands and islets, is indeed paradise for sailors. Endless islands, quiet coves, and picturesque anchoring near deserted shores – the Ionian and Aegean Seas are a yacht charterer's dream. You can also take a boat, or better yet, take a guided boating tour where you can visit one beautiful place to the other.

Sailing is one of the most common activities in Greece and the most favourite destinations are the Saronic Gulf and Cyclades. In Cyclades, you will glide by famous islands of Mykonos, Santorini, and Parikia Paros but the quiet coves of Koufonisi and Amorgos are worth the discovery where the pace is slower and the tourist louder. There is nothing quite like cruising through these clear waters; to anchor in a secluded bay, and swim/snorkel is a delight.

For those who choose an active, this you can take sailing courses or arrange a flotilla vacation, which is sort of like a cruise, but with a fleet of boats together, but not completely alone.

Watersports Galore

It is a natural progression for a country with that length of a coastline to have watersports as an extremely popular pastime. Whether you are skilled and seasoned, or you just want to enjoy the sun, and the water, you'll find it here.

There are many other activities for visitors to do, including windsurfing, kitesurfing, which are common on Paros, Naxos and Kos. Deadly Meltemi winds blowing through the Aegean provide perfect conditions for catching the wind and skimming the waves. For novices, do not despair, most coastal beaches offer one form of lesson from a school, so once you're a beginner you can get started and get moving.

If you are looking for less thrill, then kayaking is one of the most exciting ways to discover shores of Greece. Navigate, past towering cliffs, into the much deserving caverns, and in close proximity to small, deserted islands. In Crete, one can free ride on the sea along the south coast and reach beaches that cannot be accessed by any other means, only by sea. In the Ionian Islands, the water is as smooth as a mirror: just right for having an easy paddle followed by swimming.

For underwater lovers there are **scuba diving and snorkeling** in Greece also. There are numerous Niches in and around different beaches of Greek Island destinations like Zakynthos, Kefalonia and Crete you will find different sea creature including sea turtles. Discover the beauty of underwater caves and wrecks, and colourful fish and corals which make the seas of Greece so special.

Rock Climbing

For instance, if you fancy rock climbing – or if you never tried but are keen on the idea – then yep, Greece really has some great places for this! The most famous place for rock climbing is the island called Kalymnos. Renowned for its impressive limestone cliffs and vantage views of the sea, Kalymnos boasts over 3,000 recorded climbing trails: easy through to extreme. The best part? This particular area of the island has many climbing routes but with the added bonus of stunning views of the Aegean Sea is really special.

Other climbing attractions on the mainland are the immense and protruding monasteries of Meteora. These enormous, almost imaginary statues with rock pillars are crowned with monasteries, even though it is impossible to get to the top of these monasteries, there are many paths around them. What makes Meteora unique and especially attractive for rock climbers is the fact that this place is distinguished by both difficult climbs and an hours-a-day religious environment.

For the beginner, Greece has numerous climbing schools and guides who can initiate you into the pleasures of the sport – quite literally!

Biking Through Greece

If you'd rather go cycling throughout the whole area of Greece, you will not be disappointed. Cycling is gradually gaining popularity in Greece and is actually characterized by a variety of cycling tracks, including those that pass along the beautiful coastline, those that cut through the mountains. It is possible to rent bicycles nearly in all the large cities and islands and in addition there are guided bike tours if you prefer if someone will lead you.

Among those, one of the most beautiful location for cycling is the area of Peloponnese. This is the right region for cycling lovers; the rolling hills, olive groves and fantastic small villages. Cycling, you can move through the coast, through the sightseeing and places with viewing ancient ruins and having a lunch or dinner in local taverna on souvlaki or Greek salad.

If one looks for less touristy place, go to Kefalonia in the Ionian Islands. The island boasts some great hiking paths that run through meadows, gorgeous beaches, and up into the hills to offering wonderful views of the ocean. The main potential of Sidon is the deserted roads and untouched countryside – perfect for road and even mountain biking.

If you are in Crete, then you can ride through the gorge tracks or take into the mountains. Some of the trails are very challenging. Most bike rental shops on Crete also provide e-bikes which make it easier to conquer some inclines but at the same time not missing the beautiful views.

Horseback Riding

Hence where there are those who enjoy and have the tendency to drool at the sight of a horse and horse riding why would one not plan to travel within Greece in this style? Riding a horse has so much relation to mothers or with nature and if you want to ride at the best destination then Greece is the place to be.

In Rhodes, you can go horseback riding along the coastline or through the pine clad slopes of the island. It is quite fascinating to say the minimum to cycle through the countryside, and hear the sound of the ocean in the distance or smell the flowers.

Other fun is in horseback riding which is also treasured in Corfu and is even more fascinating if the ride involves the island greens. Cycle around beautiful olive tree plantations, through steep inclines, and roads which provide excellent vantage over the island and the ocean. Some will even carry you to some of the otherwise inaccessible beaches where you and your horse can swim.

While in Pelion one feels that he/she is willing to unravel history and savor nature as one cavorts on locata mule tracks that cross through picture terrene villages and forests. The area with breathtaking and beautiful green coverage and less populated pristine landscapes, is ideal for horse enthusiasts.

Skiing and Snowboarding

Greece is not a skiing country per se, however, when winter time comes, its mountain regions becomes a beautiful snow haven for winter activities. Skiing can be carried out in several ski resorts found in Greece and most of them are not more than 20km from either Athens or Thessaloniki and as such one can ski in the morning and sleep in town at night.

There are many skiing resorts in Greece and majority of these skiing resorts are famous and well developed for car access among them is Mount Parnassus which one can easily access by car for instance, from Athens, it would take 3-5hours to get. It is one of the largest skiing resorts in Greece and there are all sorts of slopes for the classifications of ski. After skiing and snowboarding, there is the nearby town of Arachova, which is locally referred as the ''Mykonos of winter.''

Another perfect place is Mount Pelion, where you can ski, seeing the sea at the same time! Despite the fact the ski resort here is relatively small that area has stunning view and thus such place may be more suitable for tourists who don't like crowded places and who would like to spend time in quite manner.

The skiing that is conducted is in northern Greece in Mount Olympus even though it lacks the rich establishments of the other skiing resorts that have fewer skiing services with few ski lifts and fewer skiing trails. Skiing on the legendary household of gods provides a feeling that is not manageable anywhere in this entire world.

Wildlife Watching
The terrains of Greece are diverse and there is vast variety of fauna found in Greece, and if you are a lover of natural world then you have lots of options to have glimpse of the animals that are inherent of this country.

If I were to list the most interesting animals you can meet in Greece, one of them would describe the loggerhead sea turtle. Zakynthos is one of the main breeding grounds of these turtles so if you are visiting the island between June and August you might be lucky to see the female turtles coming on the sand to lay eggs or young turtles hatching at night. The Marine Park of Zakynthos

At the moment, Marine Park of Zakynthos is functioning, and its main purpose is the protection of these amazing beings; there is a chance to watch turtles swimming in the island area accompanied by boats. As long as you select a proper tour operator it can be quite safe and won't cause any disturbance to the turtles.

In no this list will bird watchers miss out on Lake Kerkini in northern Greece. Artificial lake has grown to be one of the largest bird sanctuary in Europe that hosts over three hundred varieties of birds. So it is possible to view such flightless birds as brown pelican, flamingoes, heron, and in case if it is present Dalmatian pelican. It is an excellent place for a boat ride or going for a hike; you are privileged to witness what the Lord has done in providing such a view of the sight; it has high density of species of wild animals; it is awesome to be surrounded by nothing.

If your traveling destination is Pindos Mountains then you will have opportunity to meet large inhabitants of Greece, like for example, bears, wolves, and wild boars. This territory can be described as the Vikos-Aoos National Park which is a territory marked by rather severe and steep geography and some kinds of animals. Wildlife watching is possible here, and while there is no guarantee that one will see a bear there is a chance that one will at least see magnificent scenery of the wilderness.

Caving and Spelunking

Those interested in the amazingly beautiful underground landscape will not be disappointed in Greek caves that are presented here. From this, it allows me to recommend that out of all the Greek caves, Melissani Cave in Kefalonia is one the most visited cave. This is a half-submerged grotto that served as a sanctuary for the ancients Greeks and can now be visited through the sea on the vessel. Years ago the roof of the cave collapsed as well, and the whole area being lit up when the sunlight hits the water – turquoise and emerald like in fairy tale and felt like getting into a folk tale.

Another marvellous cave which is worthy of a visit is the Cave of Perama situated near Ioannina in the northwestern region of the country. It is a big natural cave with world's long surpassing one kilometer of stalactites and stalagmites. The purpose of the visit to this cave is to watch the preview of the tour, in which doors appear in front of the guests and demonstrate the creation of the cave and the rocks.

For example if you are in Crete then you have to do the Dikteon Cave because the myth says that Zeus was born from it. It has a brilliant tour with a stunning view of upland landscape. The main attraction of the cave is its big chambers and impressive cliffs.

Olive Harvesting Experiences

Greece is famous for its olives and olive oil, so why not immerse yourself in the tradition of olive harvesting? This is one of the most hands-on and rewarding outdoor activities you can enjoy in Greece, especially if you visit in the autumn months when the harvest is in full swing.

Many olive farms across the country, especially in Crete and the Peloponnese, offer visitors the chance to participate in the harvesting process. You can spend a day picking olives by hand, learning about the ancient techniques that have been used for centuries, and enjoying a traditional meal afterward. Some farms also offer olive oil tastings, where you can sample different varieties and learn how to distinguish the subtleties of flavor.

It's a fantastic way to connect with Greek culture and take home a piece of your experience (literally, since many places let you bottle your own olive oil as a souvenir).

Places You Can Go to Access These Outdoor Activities

When it comes to outdoor adventures, Greece is an endless playground. Whether you're into hiking, sailing, rock climbing, or just want to soak up the sun on a quiet beach, there's a spot for you. And while there are tons of options all over the country, some places are particularly great for specific outdoor activities. Let's take a relaxed tour through the best destinations where you can enjoy these experiences and get the most out of Greece's natural beauty.

Crete: For Hiking, Gorge Walking, and Beach Days

Crete is a massive island, so you'll find a little bit of everything here, from stunning beaches to mountains and deep gorges.

- **Hiking:** The Samaria Gorge is a highlight for hikers, stretching 16 kilometers through the White Mountains. It's a full-day adventure, starting at the Omalos Plateau and winding through towering cliffs until you reach the village of Agia Roumeli on the Libyan Sea. Along the way, you'll cross streams, walk through the Iron Gates (a narrow passage where the gorge squeezes down to just four meters wide), and pass ancient ruins.
  - **Address:** Samaria Gorge National Park, Omalos 730 05, Crete
  - **Itinerary:** Start early from Omalos, hike down to Agia Roumeli, and catch the ferry to Chora Sfakion to connect back to your starting point.

- **Beaches:** After hiking, Crete has plenty of beaches where you can unwind. Elafonissi Beach, with its pink sand and shallow waters, is perfect for a lazy day by the sea.
- **Address:** Elafonissi Beach, Elafonissi 730 01, Crete
- **Itinerary:** Drive to Elafonissi (about 1.5 hours from Chania) and spend the day lounging, swimming, and exploring nearby coves.

- **Other Activities:** Crete is also great for kayaking along the rugged southern coast. Paddle between secluded beaches, stop for a swim, and explore hidden caves. For rock climbing, Kapetaniana offers challenging climbs with views over the Asterousia Mountains and the Libyan Sea.

Santorini: For Stunning Views, Sailing, and Hiking

Santorini is famous for its caldera views and sunsets, but it's also a great base for outdoor activities.

- **Hiking:** The most popular hike on the island is the Fira to Oia trail, a cliffside path that offers breathtaking views of the caldera. The hike is about 10 kilometers and takes around three hours, depending on how often you stop to snap photos.

  - **Address: Start** from Fira (Thira), Santorini 847 00
  - **Itinerary:** Begin your hike in Fira, walking through the villages of Firostefani and Imerovigli before reaching Oia. End your day with a legendary sunset in Oia and a relaxed meal at a taverna.

- **Sailing:** There's no better way to see Santorini than from the water. You can take a sailing tour around the caldera, stopping at the island's hot springs, the volcanic Nea Kameni, and secluded beaches. Some tours even offer a BBQ lunch and a chance to snorkel in the crystal-clear waters.

  - **Address:** Santorini Old Port, Fira, Santorini 847 00
  - **Itinerary:** Book a half-day or full-day sailing tour from the Old Port. Tours typically stop at Nea Kameni, Palea Kameni (hot springs), and the Red and White Beaches.

- **Other Activities:** Santorini has some unique beaches, like the Red Beach and Perissa Beach (with its black volcanic sand), perfect for a day of lounging or snorkeling. You can also rent ATVs to explore the island's rugged landscape, riding between beaches and small villages.

Kalymnos: For Rock Climbing

Kalymnos is world-renowned for its rock climbing scene. The island's craggy cliffs, beautiful sea views, and warm climate make it a climbing paradise.

- **Rock Climbing:** Kalymnos is known as one of the best climbing destinations in the world, with over 3,000 climbing routes spread across the island. The Grande Grotta cave is a favorite for advanced climbers, but there are routes for every skill level.

  - **Address:** Kalymnos Climbing School, Masouri, Kalymnos 852 00

  - **Itinerary:** Start from Masouri, the island's climbing hub. Spend your days climbing and evenings relaxing in the village's bars and restaurants. The best climbing season is from April to October.

- **Other Activities:** When you're not climbing, Kalymnos also offers great hiking trails and opportunities for scuba diving, especially around Telendos Island.

Zakynthos: For Sea Turtles, Snorkeling, and Scenic Views

Zakynthos (or Zante) is a lush Ionian island known for its beaches, crystal-clear waters, and as a breeding ground for the endangered loggerhead sea turtle.

- **Sea Turtle Watching:** One of the most unforgettable experiences on Zakynthos is seeing loggerhead sea turtles up close. Take a boat tour from Laganas Beach or Kalamaki to Marathonisi Island (also known as Turtle Island) where you might spot turtles swimming and nesting.

 - **Address:** Laganas Beach, Laganas 290 92, Zakynthos

 - **Itinerary:** Book a half-day turtle-spotting tour and spend the afternoon snorkeling in the clear waters around Turtle Island.

- **Snorkeling and Diving:** Zakynthos is a top spot for snorkeling and diving. The Blue Caves and Keri Caves offer vibrant marine life and dramatic underwater landscapes. Dive centers on the island cater to both beginners and experienced divers.

 - **Address:** Keri Caves, Keri 290 92, Zakynthos

- **Itinerary:** Take a boat tour to the caves, where you can snorkel, dive, and swim through the azure waters.

- **Other Activities:** No trip to Zakynthos is complete without visiting Navagio Beach (also known as Shipwreck Beach). It's one of the most photographed spots in Greece, with a rusted shipwreck on a white-sand beach surrounded by towering cliffs. You can access it by boat from Porto Vromi or Agios Nikolaos.

Meteora: For Hiking and Rock Climbing

Meteora is a UNESCO World Heritage site famous for its monasteries perched atop towering rock formations. But beyond its spiritual significance, it's also an excellent spot for outdoor activities.

- **Hiking:** The trails around Meteora are stunning, offering incredible views of the monasteries and the surrounding landscape. A popular route is the Monastery Hiking Trail, which takes you up to the six active monasteries, offering panoramic views at every turn.

- **Address:** Meteora, Kalabaka 422 00

- **Itinerary:** Start your hike early to beat the heat and the crowds. Visit Great Meteoron Monastery, the largest and most famous, and end your day with a peaceful walk through the countryside.

- **Rock Climbing:** Meteora is also a fantastic place for rock climbing. The unique, smooth cliffs attract climbers from all over the world. There are routes for all levels, from beginners to advanced, and you can hire a local guide for a day of climbing amidst the striking rock formations.

- **Address:** Meteora Climbing Tours, Kalabaka 422 00

- **Itinerary:** Book a climbing tour in Kalabaka, and enjoy a day scaling the mystical rock pillars of Meteora.

Naxos: For Windsurfing and Hiking

Naxos is one of the best-kept secrets of the Cyclades, offering a mix of gorgeous beaches, historical sites, and charming villages. It's also a hotspot for windsurfing and hiking.

- **Windsurfing:** The strong winds at Mikri Vigla Beach make it one of the top windsurfing spots in Greece. The long, sandy beach has excellent conditions for both windsurfing and kitesurfing, and you'll find schools offering lessons for beginners.
  - **Address:** Mikri Vigla Beach, Mikri Vigla 843 02, Naxos
  - **Itinerary:** Spend the morning taking windsurfing lessons, and when you're ready for a break, grab lunch at a beachside taverna before heading back out on the water.

- **Hiking:** Naxos is also home to some of the best hiking trails in the Cyclades. A great route is the Mount Zas trail, which leads to the highest peak in the Cyclades. The views from the top are nothing short of spectacular, and the hike itself takes you through ancient paths and quiet villages.

  - **Address:** Start in Filoti Village, Naxos 843 02

  - **Itinerary:** Begin your hike in Filoti and follow the trail to the summit of Mount Zas. On your way back, stop in the village for a traditional meal.

Peloponnese: For Biking, Olive Harvesting, and Ancient Ruins

The Peloponnese region is a treasure trove of outdoor activities, with its combination of ancient history, rugged landscapes, and beautiful coastline. Whether you're a biking enthusiast, interested in olive harvesting, or looking to explore Greece's rich history, the Peloponnese has something for everyone.

- **Biking:** The Peloponnese is perfect for biking, offering a mix of coastal roads, quiet countryside, and challenging mountain paths. One of the best routes is the Nafplio to Epidaurus coastal ride, where you can pedal along the sparkling Saronic Gulf, passing by ancient ruins and lush landscapes.

  - **Address:** Start from Nafplio, Nafplio 211 00

  - **Itinerary:** Begin your journey in the charming seaside town of Nafplio, where you can explore its Venetian fortress. From there, ride toward Epidaurus, home to the famous ancient theatre, where you can stop and explore the ruins before continuing along the scenic coastline.

- **Olive Harvesting:** If you happen to visit during autumn, you can experience the age-old tradition of olive harvesting. The Mani Peninsula in the southern Peloponnese is one of the best places for this. Many local farms offer hands-on experiences where you can pick olives, learn about the olive oil-making process, and even taste freshly pressed oil.

- **Address:** Mani Peninsula, Peloponnese

- **Itinerary:** Book a farm stay or a day tour during the olive harvest season (typically October to November). You'll start the day in the olive groves, learn about traditional harvesting techniques, and enjoy a lunch made from local produce, including olives and olive oil.

- **Exploring Ancient Ruins:** The Peloponnese is home to some of Greece's most famous archaeological sites, like Mycenae, Olympia, and Epidaurus. For a full outdoor experience, take a guided walking tour of Mycenae, the ancient city ruled by King Agamemnon, where you'll explore the Lion's Gate and the Treasury of Atreus.

- **Address:** Mycenae Archaeological Site, Mykines 212 00

- **Itinerary:** Start your day at the Mycenae ruins, then drive to Epidaurus to see the theatre, famous for its perfect acoustics. End your day relaxing in the coastal town of Nafplio.

Rhodes: For Beach Days, Horseback Riding, and Diving

The island of Rhodes blends history with nature, offering a variety of outdoor activities, from sun-soaked beaches to scenic horseback rides and thrilling dives.

- **Beach Days:** Rhodes has some of the best beaches in Greece. Anthony Quinn Bay is a hidden gem, surrounded by rocky cliffs and pine trees, with crystal-clear waters perfect for swimming and snorkeling. For something more active, head to Faliraki Beach, where you can rent jet skis, go windsurfing, or simply relax in the sun.
  - **Address:** Anthony Quinn Bay, Kallithea 851 00, Rhodes
  - **Itinerary:** Spend the morning at Anthony Quinn Bay snorkeling or lounging on the beach. Then, head to Faliraki for water sports and a lively beach scene.

- **Horseback Riding:** For a unique way to explore Rhodes, try horseback riding along the coast. The countryside around Afandou is perfect for a peaceful ride through olive groves, open fields, and coastal trails, where you can trot along the shore as the sun sets.
  - **Address:** Afandou Beach, Afandou 851 03, Rhodes
  - **Itinerary:** Book a sunset horseback ride from a local stable. The tour typically takes you through rural Rhodes before leading you to the beach for a picturesque end to the day.
- **Diving:** Rhodes also has excellent diving spots, with shipwrecks, reefs, and underwater caves to explore. Ladiko Bay and Traganou Cave are great for beginner divers, while more experienced divers can explore deeper wrecks and reefs in the area.
  - **Address:** Ladiko Bay, Faliraki 851 00, Rhodes
  - **Itinerary:** Join a diving tour from Faliraki or Lindos. Most dive centers offer full-day excursions, with multiple dives at different sites.

Corfu: For Wildlife Watching and Sea Kayaking

Corfu, a lush Ionian island, is an excellent destination for those who love nature and outdoor activities.

- **Wildlife Watching:** Corfu's diverse landscapes make it an ideal spot for wildlife watching. The Corfu Wetlands, especially the Korission Lagoon, attract a wide range of bird species, including flamingos and herons. If you're lucky, you might also spot loggerhead turtles around the island's southern coast.

- **Address:** Korission Lagoon, Corfu 490 80

- **Itinerary:** Start your day with a guided birdwatching tour around Korission Lagoon. Bring binoculars and a camera, as you're bound to see plenty of local wildlife. Afterward, head to Issos Beach nearby for a swim and some relaxation.

- **Sea Kayaking:** Corfu's coastline is perfect for sea kayaking. One of the best routes takes you from Paleokastritsa, where you can paddle past towering cliffs, hidden caves, and isolated beaches. Stop at Paradise Beach, a quiet, pebbly cove that's only accessible by sea.

- **Address:** Paleokastritsa, Corfu 490 83

- **Itinerary:** Rent a kayak from one of the local shops in Paleokastritsa or join a guided tour. Spend a few hours paddling along the coast, stopping to snorkel or swim whenever the mood strikes.

Skiing in Mount Parnassus: For Winter Adventures

While Greece may not be the first place that comes to mind for skiing, Mount Parnassus offers some great winter sports options just a couple of hours from Athens.

89

- Skiing and Snowboarding: The Parnassos Ski Center is the largest in Greece, offering a variety of slopes for all skill levels, from beginner to advance. The resort has 23 runs, and you can rent equipment on-site or bring your own. The views from the top of the mountain are stunning, with the sea visible in the distance on clear days.

    - Address: Parnassos Ski Center, Arachova 320 04

    - Itinerary: Start your day early by driving from Athens to Arachova. Spend the day skiing or snowboarding, and after a day on the slopes, head into Arachova for dinner at a cozy taverna. If you're staying overnight, Arachova has plenty of options for a mountain village retreat.

- Other Winter Activities: If skiing isn't your thing, you can still enjoy Mount Parnassus with a snowshoeing or winter hiking tour. The surrounding Parnassos National Park is a winter wonderland during the colder months, with quiet trails and pristine snowy landscapes.

Thessaloniki: For Urban Exploring and Beach Escapes

Though it's Greece's second-largest city, Thessaloniki is close to some fantastic outdoor spots, offering a perfect mix of urban exploring and beach escapes.

- Urban Hiking: Thessaloniki itself is great for exploring on foot. Start by walking up to the Ano Poli (Upper Town), where you'll pass by traditional houses, Byzantine walls, and Ottoman structures. The views over the city and the Aegean Sea are well worth the uphill trek.

    - Address: Ano Poli, Thessaloniki 546 34

- Itinerary: Spend the morning hiking through Ano Poli. After exploring the Byzantine Walls and soaking up the views, head down to the waterfront for lunch in Ladadika.

- Beaches: If you need a break from city life, the beaches of Halkidiki are just a short drive from Thessaloniki. Kassandra and Sithonia offer a range of beaches, from lively spots with beach bars to quiet, secluded coves.
   - Address: Kassandra, Halkidiki 630 77
   - Itinerary: Rent a car and drive from Thessaloniki to Kassandra. Spend the day beach hopping or pick one of the larger beaches, like Sani Beach, to relax for the day. Finish with dinner at a seaside taverna before heading back to the city.

Indoor Activities to Enjoy and Explore in Greece

Greece is famous for its stunning beaches, ancient ruins, and outdoor adventures, but what happens when you're looking for something a little more laid-back or the weather isn't cooperating? Don't worry—Greece has plenty of indoor activities that offer just as much excitement, culture, and fun. Whether you want to dive deep into history, explore art, or even experience local traditions from the comfort of a cozy indoor space, Greece has you covered. Let's explore the indoor adventures waiting for you in this beautiful country.

Discover History in World-Class Museums

Greece is a treasure trove of history, and its museums are some of the best places to take it all in. Whether you're in Athens or exploring one of the islands, stepping into a museum is like opening a window to the past.

- **The Acropolis Museum (Athens):** If you're visiting Athens, the Acropolis Museum is an absolute must. This modern museum is located at the foot of the Acropolis hill and houses artifacts from the Acropolis site, including statues, pottery, and everyday items from ancient Greece. The museum's highlight is its top-floor Parthenon Gallery, where you can admire the famous Parthenon sculptures. As you walk through the museum, you'll be walking on glass floors that reveal the ancient city's ruins beneath your feet—a really cool touch!

  - **Address:** Dionysiou Areopagitou Street, Athens

  - **What to Do:** Spend a few hours exploring the exhibits, take in the view of the Acropolis from the museum's café, and enjoy learning about Greece's rich heritage.

- **The National Archaeological Museum (Athens):** For history buffs, the National Archaeological Museum is a dream come true. It's the largest archaeological museum in Greece and offers an incredible collection that spans prehistoric times to late antiquity. From the Mask of Agamemnon to impressive marble sculptures and ancient tools, you'll get a broad sense of ancient Greek civilization.

  - **Address:** 44 Patission Street, Athens

- **What to Do:** Wander through the different sections, focusing on areas of interest such as the Bronze Age or Classical Greece, and don't miss the ancient Greek vases!

- **Heraklion Archaeological Museum (Crete): If** you find yourself on the island of Crete, the Heraklion Archaeological Museum is the perfect place to learn about the Minoan civilization. It holds one of the most comprehensive collections of Minoan artifacts in the world, including the famous Phaistos Disc and intricately designed pottery and frescoes from the Palace of Knossos.
  - **Address:** Xanthoudidou Street, Heraklion, Crete
  - **What to Do:** Dive into the stories of King Minos and the labyrinth, and explore how Crete was once the center of Europe's earliest advanced civilization.

- **Museum of Byzantine Culture (Thessaloniki):** For a slightly different experience, the Museum of Byzantine Culture in Thessaloniki takes you on a journey through the Byzantine Empire, a period often overshadowed by ancient Greece. The museum displays religious icons, mosaics, and artifacts from churches and homes, giving you insight into this fascinating chapter of Greek history.
  - **Address:** 2 Stratou Avenue, Thessaloniki
  - **What to Do:** Spend a few hours exploring the beautiful icons and learning about Byzantine art and architecture.

Indulge in Greek Cooking Classes

If you're a foodie (and let's be real, who isn't?), taking a Greek cooking class is a fantastic indoor activity. It's the perfect way to immerse yourself in Greek culture and bring a taste of Greece back home with you.

- **Greek Cooking Class in Athens:** One of the best places to try a cooking class is right in the heart of Athens. In a cozy kitchen, you'll learn how to make some of Greece's most famous dishes—think moussaka, spanakopita (spinach pie), and tzatziki. Most classes also include a bit of local flavor, like baking traditional phyllo dough or preparing delicious baklava for dessert. At the end of the class, you'll sit down to enjoy the meal you helped create, along with a glass of local wine.

- **What to Do:** Chop, mix, and bake under the guidance of a local chef, and enjoy the fruits of your labor. Don't forget to take the recipes home!

- **Cretan Cooking Class (Chania, Crete):** Crete is known for its unique cuisine, so what better place to learn the secrets of Cretan cooking? In Chania, you can take part in a farm-to-table cooking class where you'll gather fresh ingredients from local farms and then learn how to make traditional Cretan dishes like dakos (barley rusks with tomatoes and cheese), stifado (a beef or rabbit stew), and kalitsounia (sweet cheese pastries).

- **What to Do:** Visit a farm, gather fresh produce, and cook alongside experienced Cretan cooks. The hands-on experience and rustic kitchen setting make it a warm and authentic experience.

Visit Traditional Greek Markets

If you prefer your indoor activities with a little more buzz and energy, step into one of Greece's vibrant indoor markets. They're the perfect places to get a taste of daily life in Greece while browsing for local products.

- **Varvakios Agora (Athens Central Market):** Varvakios Agora is Athens' bustling indoor market, where locals come to shop for fresh produce, meat, and fish. It's an explosion of colors, smells, and sounds. If you love food markets, this place is a must-see. You can find everything from olives and cheeses to fresh fish being sold by lively vendors. Even if you don't plan on cooking, wandering through the market is a feast for the senses.

- **Address:** Athinas Street, Athens

- **What to Do:** Stroll through the aisles, sample some fresh fruit, and take in the atmosphere. Be sure to pick up some Greek feta, honey, or herbs to take home.

- **Kapani Market (Thessaloniki):** Another fantastic market is Kapani, Thessaloniki's oldest indoor market. Here, you'll find everything from fresh produce and seafood to spices and local sweets. The market is a perfect blend of tradition and daily life, offering a more intimate look into the culinary heart of Greece's second-largest city.

- **Address:** Vlali 12, Thessaloniki

- **What to Do:** Get lost in the market's narrow aisles, chat with local vendors, and grab a snack from one of the many stalls.

Explore Greek Art Galleries

For a quieter and more reflective experience, Greek art galleries offer the perfect escape from the hustle and bustle of the streets. Whether it's modern art or ancient pottery, you'll find indoor galleries to suit every taste.

- **The National Gallery (Athens):** After a major renovation, Athens' National Gallery is back and better than ever. It's a mix of Greek art, from ancient works to contemporary masterpieces. You'll see stunning paintings from the Greek War of Independence as well as works by Modern Greek artists like Yannis Tsarouchis and Nikos Hadjikyriakos-Ghikas.

  - **Address:** 50 Vasileos Konstantinou Street, Athens

  - **What to Do:** Spend a couple of hours wandering through the various exhibitions, admiring Greece's rich artistic heritage.

- **Benaki Museum of Greek Culture (Athens):** The Benaki Museum is a wonderful spot to explore Greek culture through art and artifacts. It's not just about paintings—here, you'll find a mix of jewelry, textiles, sculptures, and ceramics that reflect Greece's diverse history, from antiquity to modern times. It's like a cultural deep dive into the country's soul.

  - **Address:** Koumpari 1, Athens

  - **What to Do:** Walk through the museum's different rooms, each telling a different part of Greece's story, and don't forget to check out the temporary exhibitions, which often showcase Modern Greek art.

- Municipal Gallery of Corfu: If you're heading to the Ionian Islands, Corfu has its own delightful art gallery that's worth checking out. The Municipal Gallery of Corfu focuses on local artists from the 19th and 20th centuries, with works that reflect the island's history and unique place in Greek culture.

　- Address: Palaia Anaktora, Corfu Town

　- What to Do: Explore the island's artistic heritage through the paintings and sculptures of Corfiot artists.

Relax in Greek Spas and Thermal Springs

If you need a break from sightseeing, Greece has a wealth of indoor spa and thermal spring options that offer relaxation and rejuvenation.

- Thermae Sylla Spa & Wellness Hotel (Evia): Located on the island of Evia, the Thermae Sylla Spa is one of Greece's most luxurious spa resorts. It uses natural thermal springs that have been known for their healing properties since ancient times. Whether you're soaking in the mineral-rich waters or enjoying a massage, you'll leave feeling completely refreshed.

　- Address: Edipsos, Evia

　- What to Do: Spend the day lounging in the thermal pools, try out a detoxifying mud treatment, or book a full body massage. If you're looking for pure indulgence, this is the place to be.

- Pozar Thermal Baths (Pella): For a more natural and rustic experience, head to the Pozar Thermal Baths in northern Greece. Located near the foothills of Mount Voras, the baths consist of both indoor and outdoor pools filled with mineral-rich hot water. While you can soak outdoors in the scenic natural environment, there are indoor facilities that offer the same rejuvenating experience, but with more privacy and comfort.

- **Address:** Loutraki, Pella
- **What to Do:** Dip into the therapeutic hot springs, take a relaxing sauna, or treat yourself to a local spa treatment.

- **Hammam Baths (Athens and Thessaloniki):** For a more traditional Greek wellness experience, visit a hammam (Turkish bath). In Athens, Hammam Baths offers a variety of services like deep cleansing steam baths, exfoliating scrubs, and massages in a beautifully restored, historic setting. In Thessaloniki, Polis Hammam offers a similar experience, perfect for unwinding after a day of exploring.

- **What to Do:** Let the steam cleanse your skin, enjoy a full-body scrub, and finish with a soothing massage. It's a unique, deeply relaxing way to tap into centuries-old Greek and Ottoman spa traditions.

Join a Local Workshop

Finally, if you're someone who likes to engage in hands-on activities while traveling, Greece offers a variety of indoor workshops where you can learn a new skill or craft.

- **Pottery Workshops (Athens & Crete):** Greek pottery is famous for its history and beauty. Join a local pottery workshop where you can learn how to shape clay into beautiful pieces inspired by ancient Greek designs. In Athens, several studios offer short workshops where you'll learn the basics of pottery making. Crete also has a long tradition of pottery, and many small towns, like Margarites, offer classes where you can make your own creations.

- **What to Do:** Spend a couple of hours getting your hands dirty, learning ancient techniques, and creating your own keepsake to take home.

- **Icon Painting Workshops (Athens, Thessaloniki, Mount Athos):** If you're interested in religious art, Greece is the perfect place to learn icon painting, an ancient art form still practiced today. There are workshops in Athens, Thessaloniki, and even on Mount Athos for those wanting to learn the traditional techniques of Byzantine iconography.

- **What to Do:** Learn how to prepare the wooden panels, mix pigments, and apply gold leaf to create your own religious icon.

Chapter Four

Hospitality in Greece

If there's one thing you'll quickly notice when you visit Greece, it's the warmth and generosity of its people. Hospitality, or philoxenia, is deeply rooted in Greek culture. This term, which translates to "friend to strangers," has been a part of Greek tradition since ancient times, where welcoming guests was considered not just a courtesy, but a moral duty. That spirit still thrives today, and you'll experience it in every corner of the country, from the bustling streets of Athens to the smallest, most remote villages.

Whether you're staying in a luxury hotel, a family-run guesthouse, or enjoying a meal in a local taverna, you'll be treated like an old friend. Greeks take pride in their hospitality, and it shows in how they greet, serve, and interact with visitors. Here's what to expect when it comes to hospitality in Greece, and how it plays a huge role in making your stay unforgettable.

The Warm Greek Welcome

From the moment you step off the plane or ferry, you'll likely be greeted with a heartfelt "kalimera!" (Good morning) or "kalos irthate!" (Welcome). Greeks love to make people feel at home, and you'll notice this in the way they offer directions, suggest hidden gems, or even invite you for a coffee.

When you're exploring Greece, you'll also find that many locals speak English, especially in tourist areas, making communication easier. But learning a few basic Greek phrases like **efharisto (thank you) or parakalo (please)** will go a long way in showing appreciation for their hospitality.

Staying in Greek Accommodations
Your stay in Greece will likely range from cozy guesthouses to luxurious resorts, and no matter where you lay your head, the hospitality will shine through. Accommodation in Greece is varied and caters to all kinds of travelers, but no matter where you stay, you'll find that the service is always personal and attentive.

Boutique Hotels and Guesthouses
In Greece, many visitors opt for small boutique hotels or family-run guesthouses. These places often provide the most authentic experience. You'll find beautifully decorated rooms, many of which reflect the local culture and architecture. What makes these stays special is the personal touch. Owners often go out of their way to make sure guests feel at home, whether that means offering home-cooked breakfasts, recommending places to visit that only locals know about, or arranging special services like guided tours or cooking classes.

For instance, if you're staying on one of the Cycladic islands, don't be surprised if the hotel owner offers you a local raki or tsipouro (local spirits) upon arrival. It's a small gesture, but it sets the tone for the relaxed, friendly atmosphere that defines Greek hospitality.

Luxurious Resorts

If you're more inclined towards a luxurious getaway, Greece has no shortage of upscale resorts, especially on islands like Santorini, Mykonos, and Crete. Here, you'll find top-notch service, with attentive staff ready to meet your every need, from bringing drinks to your poolside lounge to arranging exclusive dinners with breathtaking views of the sunset.

But even in these larger, high-end accommodations, the warmth and personal attention that is so characteristic of Greek hospitality still stands out. Don't be surprised if the resort manager introduces themselves personally or if the staff goes above and beyond to make sure your stay is perfect.

Vacation Rentals and Apartments

For a more laid-back and independent experience, vacation rentals, apartments, and Airbnb options are plentiful across Greece. These are ideal for families or groups looking to immerse themselves in the local atmosphere at their own pace. Often, these rentals are managed by locals who will still make the effort to welcome you with a smile, share tips on the best restaurants or beaches, and even leave some homemade goodies in the kitchen.

Greek Food: More than Just a Meal

In Greece, food is so much more than a way to satisfy hunger. It's a social experience, a time to connect with others and celebrate life. Whether you're sitting down for a long lunch in a seaside taverna or enjoying a traditional meal at someone's home, you'll quickly understand that food and hospitality go hand in hand in Greece.

Tavernas and Family-Run Restaurants

The quintessential Greek taverna is more than just a place to eat—it's a social hub. These family-run establishments serve up homemade dishes with recipes passed down through generations. From grilled meats and fresh seafood to rich stews and crispy saganaki (fried cheese), everything is cooked with love, and often using ingredients grown or sourced locally. Don't be surprised if the owner comes out of the kitchen to greet you, recommend dishes, or pour you a glass of wine. In smaller tavernas, it's common for the cook (who might also be the owner) to chat with customers about the menu, explaining what's fresh that day or how a particular dish is made.

A Meze Feast

One of the most delightful aspects of dining in Greece is the concept of meze—small plates of food shared by everyone at the table. Think of it as the Greek version of tapas. Meze dishes range from olives, cheese, and dips like tzatziki to grilled octopus, fried calamari, and roasted vegetables. Eating meze is a communal experience and a great way to try a little bit of everything.

Greeks take their time during meals, savoring each bite, and it's common for meals to stretch for hours, especially when accompanied by lively conversation and a glass of local wine or ouzo. You'll never feel rushed, and more often than not, your hosts will encourage you to relax and enjoy the experience.

Dining at a Greek Home

If you're fortunate enough to be invited to a local's home for a meal, consider it an honor. Greeks love to entertain, and they'll pull out all the stops to make sure their guests feel welcome. Expect to be treated to a feast of homemade dishes like moussaka, souvlaki, or gemista (stuffed vegetables), often made with ingredients from their own garden.

You'll likely be offered more food than you can handle, and saying "no" can be tricky as your host will insist that you have seconds, thirds, and maybe even fourths! It's all part of the generous Greek spirit, and while your stomach might be protesting, it's hard to resist the delicious flavors.

The Role of Coffee and Dessert in Greek Culture

Coffee in Greece is more than just a caffeine fix—it's a way of life. Greeks love to sit and chat over coffee, and coffeehouses, or kafeneia, are central to daily life. Whether it's a morning cup of strong Greek coffee or an afternoon freddo cappuccino (iced cappuccino), the act of sipping coffee is often paired with good conversation and people-watching.

The Greek Coffee Culture

One of the most traditional drinks is Greek coffee, served in a small cup and brewed to a frothy finish. It's meant to be sipped slowly, and usually accompanied by a glass of water. When you're sitting in a café or kafeneio, time seems to slow down, and this is very much the point. Greeks use coffee breaks to catch up with friends, debate current events, or simply relax.

Sweet Treats

Of course, no coffee break is complete without something sweet on the side. In Greece, dessert plays an important role in hospitality. After a meal, it's common for a complimentary dessert to arrive at your table—usually something simple, like fresh fruit, loukoumades (Greek doughnuts drizzled with honey), or baklava. Even in casual restaurants, you'll often be treated to a sweet gesture from the kitchen, as a way of saying "thank you" for dining with them.

Festivals and Celebrations

Greece's hospitality truly shines during festivals and celebrations. These events bring people together in a communal spirit of joy, where food, music, and dancing play a big role. If you happen to be in Greece during a local festival, be prepared to be swept up in the festivities.

Easter in Greece

Easter is the most important holiday in Greece, and the celebrations are a testament to Greek hospitality. It's a time when families gather, but it's also common for neighbors, friends, and even visitors to be invited to join in the feast. After the midnight church service, the celebrations kick off with a meal that includes lamb, magiritsa soup, and plenty of wine.

Local Festivals (Panigyria)

Many towns and villages hold festivals, or panigyria, in honor of their patron saints. These events are often open to everyone, and locals will welcome you to eat, dance, and celebrate with them. You'll find tables piled high with traditional dishes, live music playing well into the night, and a lively atmosphere that's all about community spirit.

Embracing Greek Hospitality: Tips for Travelers

To make the most of Greece's legendary hospitality, there are a few things to keep in mind that will help you connect with locals and truly embrace the experience.

- **Learn a Few Greek Phrases:** While many Greeks speak English, especially in tourist areas, making an effort to speak a few words of Greek can go a long way. Simple phrases like yassou (hello), efharisto (thank you), and parakalo (please/you're welcome) are always appreciated and show respect for the local culture.

- **Be Open to Invitations:** Greeks are known for their spontaneity. You might be invited for a coffee, a meal, or even a celebration by someone you've just met. If you're comfortable, embrace these invitations—they often lead to the most memorable experiences.

- **Don't Rush:** Greek hospitality is about enjoying the moment, so don't be in a hurry. Whether it's sitting down for a long meal or taking time to chat with someone you've just met, let yourself slow down and appreciate the leisurely pace of life.

- **Give Back:** Hospitality is a two-way street. While Greeks are incredibly generous, it's always good to reciprocate in small ways. Bringing a small gift to your host, offering to help with a meal, or simply expressing your gratitude goes a long way.

- **Respect Local Customs:** While Greece is a relaxed and welcoming country, it's important to be mindful of local customs and traditions, especially in more rural areas. For instance, dressing modestly when visiting churches or participating in religious festivals is a sign of respect.

Hospitality during Greek Holidays

If you visit Greece during one of its major holidays, like Easter or Christmas, you'll get a front-row seat to some of the country's most deeply rooted traditions of hospitality. These holidays are often a time of open doors, where families, neighbors, and even strangers come together to celebrate.

Easter Celebrations

Greek Easter, in particular, is a time when hospitality reaches its peak. It's the most significant holiday in Greece, celebrated with elaborate feasts, church services, and lots of family gatherings. Visitors are often welcomed to join in the celebrations, whether that's sharing a meal of roasted lamb after the midnight church service or being invited to crack red-dyed eggs as part of the Easter tradition.

Christmas in Greece

Christmas in Greece is another wonderful time to experience hospitality at its finest. Families gather for festive meals, and the tradition of offering sweets like **melomakarona (honey cookies) and kourabiedes (butter cookies)** is a way of spreading cheer. If you're visiting Greece during this time, expect to be offered these treats wherever you go, whether it's at a hotel, restaurant, or someone's home.

Mountain and Countryside Retreats: Serenity Away from the Coast

For travelers who prefer the mountains over the beach, Greece's interior offers some spectacular countryside and mountain retreats. These accommodations give you a chance to disconnect and soak up the natural beauty, often in charming villages or surrounded by lush landscapes.

Stone Houses in Zagorohoria

In northern Greece, the Zagorohoria region is a cluster of traditional stone-built villages set against a backdrop of rugged mountains and deep gorges. Staying in a stone guesthouse here, like Papigo Towers or Mikro Papigo 1700, allows you to experience the tranquility of the Greek mountains. With their cozy fireplaces, wooden accents, and breathtaking views, these mountain lodges are perfect for nature lovers and those seeking a quiet escape. Plus, there are endless hiking trails and activities like river rafting and horseback riding to keep you busy during the day.

Meteora Monastery Guesthouses

One of the most unique and awe-inspiring places to stay in Greece is near the Meteora monasteries. The towering rock formations, topped with centuries-old monasteries, create a surreal landscape. You can stay in nearby guesthouses or boutique hotels like Doupiani House, which offers panoramic views of Meteora. Waking up in this mystical setting feels like stepping into another world, and the area's hiking trails and monasteries make it a perfect place for both adventure and reflection.

Island Hopping and Staying on Boats: A Floating Hotel

For those who crave a little more adventure, why not turn your accommodation into a floating hotel? Sailing between Greece's islands offers an entirely different way to experience the country, and you can do it without ever leaving your room—or boat, in this case.

Chartering a Yacht

Island hopping on a private yacht is one of the most luxurious and flexible ways to explore the Greek islands. Whether you sail through the Cyclades or explore the more remote Dodecanese islands, chartering a yacht lets you wake up in a different spot every morning. Some companies offer fully crewed yachts with a captain and chef, ensuring a truly relaxing experience. You can spend your days lounging on deck, snorkeling in hidden coves, and dining under the stars, all from the comfort of your floating accommodation.

Sleep Aboard in Athens

If you don't want to commit to a full yacht charter, you can still enjoy life on the water by staying aboard a boat moored in one of Greece's many marinas. In places like Alimos Marina in Athens, you'll find sailboats and yachts available for overnight stays. These offer a unique perspective on the city, allowing you to relax on the water after a day of sightseeing.

Chapter Five

Accommodations in Greece: Top Hotels, Guest Houses, Airbnbs, Inns, and More

When planning a trip to Greece, the place you choose to stay can set the tone for your entire experience. The beauty of traveling here is that there's something for everyone—whether you prefer the comforts of a luxury hotel, the charm of a cozy guesthouse, or the freedom of an Airbnb. Each type of accommodation comes with its own vibe, so no matter your style, you'll find something that feels just right.

From bustling city stays to serene island retreats, let's explore the wide variety of places to stay in Greece that make your trip as comfortable as possible.

Hotels: From Luxury to Budget-Friendly Comfort

Whether you're seeking high-end amenities or just a simple room to crash in after a day of exploring, hotels in Greece come in all shapes and sizes. The key is knowing what you're after—whether it's five-star luxury or a more budget-friendly option.

Luxury Hotels: Spoil Yourself

Greece is home to some seriously luxurious hotels that go above and beyond when it comes to pampering their guests. If you're the type who enjoys unwinding in infinity pools, indulging in spa treatments, and sipping cocktails while watching the sunset over the Aegean, luxury hotels are your go-to. Islands like Santorini, Mykonos, and Crete are known for their upscale resorts that combine modern elegance with the beauty of traditional Cycladic architecture.

In Santorini, for example, hotels like **Canaves Oia** Suites offer stunning caldera views, private plunge pools, and high-end dining. Imagine waking up each morning to the sight of the blue sea stretching out before you, while enjoying a made-to-order breakfast delivered to your room.

Athens also has its fair share of luxury spots, such as the **Hotel Grande Bretagne**, which offers unbeatable views of the Acropolis and a rooftop pool to cool off after a hot day of sightseeing. Staying here, you get the best of both worlds: high-class service and proximity to all the major landmarks.

Boutique Hotels: Small, Stylish, and Personal

If you're after something a bit more intimate, boutique hotels are a wonderful choice. These small, independent hotels are known for their attention to detail and personalized service. You'll often find them in unique settings, like renovated mansions or charming village homes. Many are decorated with local flair, combining modern comforts with traditional Greek style.

Boutique hotels in places like **Naxos, Paros, and Hydra** tend to be family-owned, giving you a warm and personalized touch. Plus, these places often provide insider tips on where to go and what to see, helping you experience the more authentic side of the islands.

Budget-Friendly Hotels: Affordable, Yet Comfortable

Don't worry if you're traveling on a budget. Greece has plenty of affordable hotels that offer clean, comfortable rooms without breaking the bank. You'll find budget options across the mainland and islands, especially in cities like Athens and Thessaloniki or on lesser-known islands like Naxos and Tinos. These hotels may not have the same level of luxury, but they'll often surprise you with their charm, friendly service, and convenient locations.

Take the **Hotel Argo in Piraeus**, for example. It's simple and cozy, but perfectly located for travelers catching an early ferry. These types of hotels are perfect if you plan on spending most of your time out and about, and just need a comfy spot to rest at night.

Guest Houses: Homely and Welcoming

Guest houses in Greece are a fantastic option if you're looking for a more personal experience. Often family-run, these stays make you feel like you're staying with friends rather than just renting a room. They're cozy, welcoming, and often located in beautiful, traditional houses that have been passed down through generations.

Island Guest Houses

On the islands, guest houses give you the chance to live like a local. These small, intimate stays often come with rooms decorated in traditional Greek style—think whitewashed walls, blue accents, and handcrafted wooden furniture. In places **like Syros or Ikaria**, the owners might even invite you to join them for a homemade meal or recommend hidden beaches only locals know about.

Take **Villa Konstantin in Mykonos** as an example. It's a family-owned guesthouse that feels more like staying with a warm host than a commercial establishment. It's not uncommon for the owners to greet you with a local drink like raki or tsipouro, and by the end of your stay, you'll likely feel like part of the family.

Mountain and Village Guest Houses

If you're venturing into the mountainous areas, like Zagorohoria in northern Greece or Pelion, guest houses offer a peaceful retreat surrounded by nature. These guest houses are often located in stone buildings with cozy fireplaces for the cooler months and stunning views of the surrounding landscape.

In Metsovo, for example, a guest house might offer homemade jams and traditional cheeses for breakfast, along with tips on the best hiking routes in the nearby Pindos Mountains. These stays are perfect for those looking to escape the crowds and experience the quieter, more authentic side of Greece.

Airbnbs: Your Home Away from Home

If you prefer to have a space all to yourself, booking an Airbnb in Greece gives you the freedom to come and go as you please while feeling at home. This option is ideal for families, groups, or travelers looking for a longer stay, as you can find entire apartments or houses, often with full kitchens and plenty of space.

City Airbnbs: Live Like a Local

In cities like Athens and Thessaloniki, Airbnb rentals are plentiful. You can stay in a sleek, modern apartment in the heart of the action or a quieter neighborhood with a more local vibe. Athens neighborhoods like Koukaki or Exarchia offer plenty of Airbnb options, putting you close to restaurants, bars, and all the city's main attractions.

What's great about staying in an Airbnb is that it allows you to live like a local. You can pop into the nearby bakery for fresh bread in the morning or visit the local market to pick up ingredients for a home-cooked meal. Plus, with the variety of styles available, you can pick something that suits your taste, whether it's a modern loft or a cozy, traditional apartment.

Airbnbs on the Islands

On the islands, Airbnbs range from simple studios to luxurious villas with private pools. Booking a stay in an Airbnb on islands like Corfu or Rhodes allows you to experience the local way of life while enjoying all the privacy you could want. Many Airbnbs come with stunning sea views, and you'll often have your own outdoor space to enjoy the sunshine in peace. Imagine staying in a small apartment in **Plaka on Naxos**, just a short walk from the beach, or renting a rustic stone house in Chania, Crete, where you can have a glass of wine on your own private terrace as the sun sets.

Inns: Quaint and Full of Character

Inns are another option for travelers seeking a cozy, welcoming stay. Inns in Greece are often smaller, charming establishments, typically located in historical buildings or family homes. They provide a more intimate experience than hotels, but with a bit more structure and service than you'd find at an Airbnb or guest house.

Historic Inns in Athens and Thessaloniki

In Greece's major cities, inns tend to have a lot of history and character. They're often found in old neoclassical buildings, with rooms that have been lovingly restored while maintaining their original charm. Take the **Athens Gate Hotel**, for example, which offers modern comfort with views of ancient ruins right from your room. These types of inns often have fewer rooms, creating a more intimate atmosphere that makes you feel like you're stepping back in time.

Seaside Inns on the Islands

If you're headed to the islands, staying at a seaside inn is a great way to enjoy the beach while still having easy access to local shops and restaurants. Inns in places like Nafplio or Hydra offer a balance between modern comfort and historical charm. You'll find friendly service, beautifully decorated rooms, and the chance to wake up to the sound of the waves.

Eco-Friendly Stays: Sleep Green

If you care about sustainability and want to minimize your environmental footprint, Greece has a growing number of eco-friendly accommodations. These places focus on using renewable energy, reducing waste, and sourcing local, organic products.

Eco-Resorts on Crete

On Crete, eco-friendly resorts like **Milia Mountain Retreat** have made sustainability a priority. Milia, for example, is powered entirely by renewable energy, and the food served comes straight from the surrounding land. Staying at places like this allows you to enjoy Greece's natural beauty without harming the environment.

Eco-Friendly Guesthouses

In other parts of Greece, you'll find small guesthouses and boutique hotels that take sustainability seriously. These might use solar power, recycle water, or offer organic toiletries. Some even have gardens where they grow their own vegetables and herbs, which you can enjoy in the meals they serve.

No matter what kind of accommodation you're looking for in Greece, there's something that will suit your style, budget, and sense of adventure. Whether it's a luxurious hotel with endless sea views, a cozy guesthouse tucked away in a mountain village, or an Airbnb where you can make yourself at home, Greece's wide range of accommodations guarantees that you'll find the perfect place to stay.

Chapter Six
Things to Eat in Greece

One of the true joys of visiting Greece is, without a doubt, the food. Greeks don't just eat to live—they live to eat, and every meal is an event. Whether you're sitting down to a multi-course feast in a seaside taverna or grabbing a quick snack from a street vendor, there's something special about the flavors of Greece. Fresh ingredients, simple recipes, and a whole lot of love go into every bite. And trust me, once you've had a taste of real Greek food, you'll never look at a salad or a piece of grilled meat the same way again.

Let's dig into some of the must-try dishes and snacks that make Greek cuisine so memorable.

Meze: Small Plates, Big Flavor

One of the most delightful ways to eat in Greece is by sharing meze—small plates of food that are perfect for grazing over with a glass of wine or ouzo. Meze is all about variety. These little dishes are packed with flavor, and they give you a chance to try a bit of everything.

Tzatziki: This refreshing dip is a staple of Greek cuisine. Made with thick, creamy yogurt, cucumber, garlic, and a touch of olive oil, it's served chilled and pairs perfectly with pita bread or vegetables. It's light, fresh, and a great way to start any meal.

Feta Cheese: You can't talk about Greek food without mentioning feta. This tangy, crumbly cheese is made from sheep or goat's milk and is often served drizzled with olive oil and sprinkled with oregano. Whether it's in a salad or as a stand-alone snack, feta adds a burst of flavor to everything.

Saganaki: This is fried cheese—yes, you read that right. A slab of cheese (usually kefalograviera) is pan-fried until it's golden and crispy on the outside but soft and melty on the inside. It's served hot, often with a squeeze of lemon, and it's one of those dishes that you'll find hard to stop eating once you start.

Dolmades: These are little parcels of vine leaves stuffed with a mix of rice, herbs, and sometimes meat. They're served cold and have a tangy, lemony flavor that's both refreshing and satisfying.

Keftedes: Greek meatballs, or keftedes, are a great little bite. Made with ground meat (usually beef or lamb), herbs, and spices, they're fried to perfection and served with tzatziki or alongside some freshly baked bread.

Fava: This creamy dip is made from yellow split peas and has a rich, velvety texture. It's often topped with olive oil, onions, or capers and is best enjoyed with crusty bread.

The Greek Salad: Fresh, Simple, Delicious

You might think you know Greek salad, but nothing beats the real deal when you're in Greece. This classic dish, known as horiatiki, is made with the freshest ingredients—juicy tomatoes, crisp cucumbers, green peppers, onions, Kalamata olives, and, of course, a big chunk of feta on top. It's drizzled with olive oil and sprinkled with oregano, and that's all it needs. No lettuce, no extra dressing—just simple, honest flavors. The combination of sweet, salty, and tangy hits all the right notes, making it the perfect side dish or even a meal on its own during a hot summer day.

Street Food: Grab and Go Greek Style

While Greece is full of sit-down restaurants and tavernas, some of the best food can be found right on the street. Greek street food is fast, tasty, and often comes wrapped in a piece of warm pita bread.

Gyro: This is probably the most well-known street food in Greece. Gyro is made with meat (usually pork or chicken) that's slow-cooked on a vertical rotisserie. It's sliced thin and served in pita bread along with tomatoes, onions, fries, and a generous dollop of tzatziki. It's the perfect on-the-go meal that's filling and full of flavor.

Souvlaki: Similar to gyro, souvlaki is made from grilled skewers of meat, often pork, lamb, or chicken. The skewers are sometimes served in pita with the same fillings as a gyro, or they can be eaten straight off the stick with a side of salad or fries. Either way, it's one of the simplest yet most delicious things you'll eat in Greece.

Loukoumades: If you're in the mood for something sweet, look for a stand selling loukoumades. These bite-sized doughnuts are fried until golden and crispy, then drizzled with honey and sprinkled with cinnamon or chopped nuts. They're light, fluffy, and totally addictive.

Koulouri: For something quick and easy in the morning, grab a koulouri—a circular bread ring coated in sesame seeds. It's a simple, satisfying snack that's especially good with a cup of Greek coffee.

Seafood: Fresh from the Aegean

With so much coastline, it's no surprise that Greece is a seafood lover's paradise. Whether you're dining at a seaside taverna or enjoying a more upscale meal, the seafood in Greece is incredibly fresh and often simply prepared to let the natural flavors shine.

Grilled Octopus: One of the most iconic Greek seafood dishes is grilled octopus. The octopus is tenderized, grilled over an open flame, and served with just a drizzle of olive oil and a squeeze of lemon. The result is smoky, tender, and full of flavor—a must-try for seafood fans.

Fried Calamari: Another popular dish is kalamarakia tiganita—fried calamari. The squid is lightly battered and fried until golden, then served with a wedge of lemon. It's crispy, light, and delicious, especially when paired with a cold glass of white wine or ouzo.

Garides Saganaki (Shrimp Saganaki): Shrimp saganaki is shrimp cooked in a rich tomato sauce with garlic, herbs, and feta cheese. The combination of flavors is heavenly, and it's usually served with bread to mop up every last drop of that savory sauce.

Lobster Pasta (Astakomakaronada): If you're feeling fancy, try astakomakaronada—lobster pasta. This dish is a Greek favorite on islands like Mykonos and Santorini. The lobster is cooked in a tomato and wine sauce, then tossed with spaghetti. It's rich, decadent, and perfect for a special night out.

Traditional Greek Dishes You Can't Miss

Beyond meze and street food, there are plenty of hearty traditional Greek dishes that will make your mouth water. These are the types of meals that stick with you long after your trip ends, and you'll likely find yourself craving them back home.

Moussaka: One of Greece's most famous dishes, moussaka is a baked casserole made with layers of eggplant, potatoes, minced meat (usually lamb or beef), and a creamy béchamel sauce. It's rich, hearty, and comforting—a bit like a Greek version of lasagna. It's best eaten fresh out of the oven, when the flavors are at their peak.

Pastitsio: Similar to moussaka but with a pasta twist, pastitsio is made with layers of pasta, ground meat, and béchamel sauce, all baked together into a deliciously comforting dish. It's like a Greek-style baked ziti, and it's one of those meals that leaves you feeling full and satisfied.

Stifado: This is a slow-cooked stew made with beef or rabbit, onions, garlic, red wine, and tomatoes. The meat becomes incredibly tender, and the sauce is rich and flavorful. It's a perfect dish to warm you up on a cooler evening.

Gemista: If you're looking for something a little lighter but still packed with flavor, try gemista. These are tomatoes or bell peppers stuffed with rice, herbs, and sometimes meat, then baked until soft and bursting with flavor. They're usually served with a side of potatoes and are a great vegetarian option.

Spanakopita: This spinach pie is a popular snack or appetizer, made with layers of flaky phyllo dough filled with spinach and feta cheese. It's crispy on the outside, warm and savory on the inside, and always delicious.

Greek Desserts: Sweet Endings
No meal in Greece is complete without something sweet to finish it off. Greek desserts are often simple but satisfying, with many featuring honey, nuts, and flaky layers of phyllo dough.

Baklava: Probably the most famous Greek dessert, baklava is a sticky-sweet treat made from layers of phyllo dough, honey, and chopped nuts.

It's crispy, sticky, and utterly irresistible. One bite and you'll understand why this dessert has been loved for centuries.

Galaktoboureko: This is a custard-filled pastry made with layers of crispy phyllo dough, baked until golden, and then soaked in a sweet syrup. The creamy custard and crunchy pastry make for a heavenly combination.

Kataifi: Similar to baklava but with a unique twist, kataifi is made with shredded phyllo dough instead of layers, giving it a unique texture. It's filled with a mixture of nuts, usually walnuts or pistachios, and then soaked in a sweet honey syrup. The combination of crunchy, shredded phyllo and sticky sweetness makes kataifi a delightful treat that's both familiar and different from its baklava cousin.

Loukoumades: We mentioned these earlier in the street food section, but they definitely deserve a spot here too. Loukoumades are bite-sized Greek doughnuts, fried until golden, then drenched in honey and sprinkled with cinnamon or nuts. They're light, crispy on the outside, and fluffy on the inside—perfect for sharing (or not).

Melomakarona: These are honey-soaked cookies, traditionally made during the holiday season, but you'll often find them year-round in bakeries. Made with flour, olive oil, and spices like cinnamon and clove, they're baked until golden and then dipped in a honey syrup before being sprinkled with walnuts. The result is a soft, sticky, and wonderfully spiced cookie.

Rizogalo (Rice Pudding): If you're a fan of creamy desserts, rizogalo is Greece's take on rice pudding. It's made with rice, milk, sugar, and a hint of cinnamon. It's often served cold, making it a refreshing and comforting dessert that's not too heavy.

Drinks: What to Sip While You Snack

Of course, no discussion of food in Greece would be complete without mentioning the drinks that accompany these delicious dishes. Whether you're sipping something to cool you off during a hot day or enjoying a strong digestif after a meal, Greek drinks are as much a part of the culinary experience as the food.

Ouzo: The national drink of Greece, ouzo is a clear, anise-flavored spirit that's often enjoyed as an aperitif. It's typically served with meze, and the proper way to drink it is to add a splash of water or ice, which turns the clear liquid cloudy. It has a strong licorice flavor, so it's definitely an acquired taste, but sipping ouzo in the afternoon sun is a quintessential Greek experience.

Raki/Tsipouro: In Crete, you'll find locals sipping raki, a clear, potent spirit made from distilled grapes. Similar to tsipouro, which is found on the mainland, it's often offered as a welcome drink or as a gesture of hospitality at the end of a meal. Be warned—it's strong! But it's usually served with small bites of food to take the edge off.

Greek Coffee: Greek coffee is similar to Turkish coffee, made in a small pot called a briki and served in tiny cups. It's thick, strong, and has a layer of fine coffee grounds at the bottom. Don't try to drink those! Instead, sip slowly and enjoy the strong flavor. Greek coffee is traditionally sipped slowly, often with a glass of water on the side. It's perfect for a late morning or afternoon break.

Frappe: If you need something to cool you down, especially during the summer, order a frappe. This iced coffee drink is made with instant coffee, sugar, and milk (if you like), all shaken up and served over ice. It's the drink of choice for many Greeks on a hot day, and it's a great pick-me-up when you're wandering the streets or relaxing at a beach café.

Wine: Greece is one of the world's oldest wine producers, and the country's unique climate and terrain create some really interesting and flavorful wines. Assyrtiko is a popular white wine from Santorini, known for its crisp and mineral taste, while Agiorgitiko is a rich red wine from the Peloponnese. Many restaurants will offer local wines by the glass or carafe, giving you the chance to try regional varieties without breaking the bank.

Seasonal and Regional Specialties

Greece's food scene is strongly influenced by the seasons and the region you're in. This means that the best dishes change depending on when and where you visit, giving you a fresh and unique culinary experience every time.

Crete: A Food Lover's Paradise

Crete, Greece's largest island, is known for its incredible food. The island's cuisine is rustic, hearty, and focused on fresh, local ingredients. Some standout dishes include:

Dakos: Often called the "Greek bruschetta," dakos is a Cretan specialty made with barley rusks topped with chopped tomatoes, crumbled feta or mizithra cheese, olives, and a drizzle of olive oil. It's simple, but the flavors are fresh and vibrant.

Cretan Honey: The Island's honey is famous for its rich, floral flavor. Be sure to try some, either on its own or drizzled over yogurt.

Lamb with Stamnagathi: This dish features tender lamb cooked with stamnagathi, a type of wild greens that grow on the island. The greens are slightly bitter, but when paired with the savory lamb, it creates a beautifully balanced dish.

Northern Greece: Hearty and Rich

In the north, the cuisine tends to be a bit heartier, with rich stews, grilled meats, and plenty of spices. Some dishes you might come across include:

Bougatsa: A popular breakfast pastry, bougatsa is made with layers of phyllo dough filled with custard, cheese, or minced meat. It's usually sprinkled with powdered sugar and cinnamon when served sweet, and it's a great way to start the day.

Kasseri Cheese: Northern Greece is known for its cheeses, and kasseri is one of the best. It's a semi-hard cheese with a mild, buttery flavor, often enjoyed with bread or melted over meats and vegetables.

The Peloponnese: A Taste of Tradition

In the Peloponnese, you'll find traditional Greek dishes prepared with local ingredients, from the famous Kalamata olives to sweet, juicy oranges. One dish to look out for:

Hilopites: A traditional type of Greek pasta, hilopites are often made with fresh eggs and milk. They're usually served with a rich tomato sauce or tossed with browned butter and cheese, making for a simple but flavorful meal.

Best Places to Eat in Greece

When you visit Greece, food isn't just fuel for your adventures—it's an essential part of the experience. Whether you're indulging in a long, leisurely meal at a seaside taverna, enjoying street food on the go, or dining at a stylish restaurant in the heart of Athens, you'll find that food in Greece is a reflection of its culture—vibrant, warm, and full of life. Greek cuisine is a celebration of fresh ingredients, time-honored recipes, and shared moments, making every meal special.

Athens: Where Tradition Meets Trend

As the capital, Athens is a bustling city full of contrasts. It's where ancient ruins coexist with a modern food scene that's always evolving. You'll find everything from family-run tavernas serving classic dishes to trendy restaurants pushing the boundaries of Greek cuisine.

1. Varoulko Seaside

For seafood lovers, Varoulko Seaside is a must-visit. Located in the picturesque Mikrolimano marina, this Michelin-starred restaurant offers some of the best seafood in the city. Chef Lefteris Lazarou, one of the most celebrated chefs in Greece, creates innovative dishes like shrimp in a rich tomato sauce with feta or octopus carpaccio. The setting by the water makes it perfect for a romantic dinner as the sun sets over the sea.

2. Oineas Restaurant

If you're exploring the lively Psiri neighborhood, you'll stumble upon Oineas, a cozy spot with a welcoming vibe. This place offers traditional Greek comfort food with a twist. Think of slow-cooked lamb with herbs, grilled halloumi, and creamy moussaka. The restaurant's rustic decor and friendly service make it feel like you're dining in someone's home.

3. Avli

Hidden away in the heart of Athens, Avli is a little oasis. This charming taverna is tucked into a quiet courtyard, giving you a break from the city's hustle. The menu is simple but delicious, with dishes like grilled meats, stuffed tomatoes, and refreshing Greek salad. It's the perfect spot for a relaxed lunch or dinner with friends.

4. Ta Karamanlidika Tou Fani

For something a bit more casual but no less tasty, head to Ta Karamanlidika Tou Fani, a deli-turned-restaurant that focuses on meats and cheeses. The place offers a feast of cold cuts, sausages, and cheeses from around Greece, served with fresh bread and olives. You can sit down to a platter of goodies or grab something quick to go. Either way, it's a great spot to experience local flavors in a relaxed, unfussy setting.

Thessaloniki: A Culinary Melting Pot

Known as the cultural capital of Greece, Thessaloniki is famous for its rich history and incredible food scene. The city's cuisine reflects its past as a meeting point for different cultures, resulting in a unique blend of flavors and influences.

1. Mourga

If you're in the mood for seafood with a modern twist, Mourga is the place to be. This small, unassuming restaurant in the city center is known for its creative dishes and fresh ingredients. The menu changes based on what's in season, but you might find delicacies like grilled sardines, seafood risotto, or prawns with lemon and herbs. It's casual, it's cool, and the food is always outstanding.

2. Extravaganza

In Thessaloniki's trendy neighborhoods, you'll find spots like Extravaganza, where young chefs are pushing boundaries. This restaurant offers a modern take on traditional Greek dishes with a focus on high-quality, locally-sourced ingredients. Think roasted lamb with yogurt sauce, smoked mackerel, or a surprising twist on fava (yellow split pea dip). It's the kind of place where you'll want to order one of everything.

3. Sempriko

For a truly local experience, head to Sempriko, a laid-back restaurant that specializes in Greek charcuterie. You'll find a wide range of cured meats, cheeses, and other products sourced from small producers around the country. Their platters are perfect for sharing, paired with Greek wines and house-made bread. It's a fantastic spot for a casual, flavorful meal in a warm, welcoming atmosphere.

Crete: Rich Flavors of the Mediterranean

Crete is the largest of the Greek islands and has a food culture all its own. Known for its fresh produce, olive oil, and wild greens, the cuisine here is rustic, hearty, and full of flavor. Eating in Crete feels like a deep dive into the heart of Mediterranean cooking.

1. Peskesi (Heraklion)

If you want to experience traditional Cretan cuisine at its best, Peskesi is a must. This restaurant in Heraklion prides itself on using local, organic ingredients to recreate age-old recipes. From slow-cooked lamb to stuffed vine leaves and their signature dakos (a Cretan-style bruschetta), everything here is a celebration of the island's natural bounty. The atmosphere is cozy, with a mix of rustic charm and modern comfort.

2. Tamam (Chania)

Located in the picturesque city of Chania, Tamam is housed in an old Turkish bath and offers a unique dining experience. The menu features a blend of Cretan and Middle Eastern flavors, a nod to the island's history. Expect dishes like moussaka, grilled meats, and seafood, all prepared with a Mediterranean twist. The restaurant is always buzzing with energy, making it a great place to immerse yourself in the local vibe.

3. Thalassino Ageri (Chania)

For those who love fresh seafood, Thalassino Ageri offers a dreamy setting right by the water. It's a bit off the beaten path, but the food is worth the journey. You'll dine with your feet practically in the sand, enjoying dishes like grilled octopus, fish soup, and calamari, all served with simple sides like boiled greens and olive oil. It's a truly authentic Cretan dining experience.

The Cyclades: Island Hopping and Dining

The Cyclades, including islands like Santorini, Mykonos, and Naxos, are some of the most famous Greek islands, not only for their stunning landscapes but also for their culinary delights. Each island has its own specialties, so island hopping means sampling something new at every stop.

1. Selene (Santorini)

Santorini is known for its breathtaking views and excellent food, and Selene is a shining example of both. This fine-dining restaurant focuses on contemporary Greek cuisine with an emphasis on local ingredients. Dishes like fava bean puree, white eggplant salad, and fresh seafood highlight the flavors of the island. The restaurant also offers wine pairings featuring Santorini's unique volcanic wines, making the experience even more special.

2. Kiki's Tavern (Mykonos)

For something more laid-back, Kiki's Tavern on Mykonos is a local favorite. This no-frills, beachside taverna is known for its grilled meats and fresh salads. The restaurant doesn't take reservations, and there's often a line, but the wait is part of the experience. You can grab a glass of wine and relax by the beach while you wait. Once seated, expect plates of juicy pork chops, grilled vegetables, and fresh fish served in the most charmingly simple setting.

3. Metaxi Mas (Santorini)

If you're looking for a hidden gem, head to Metaxi Mas in the village of Exo Gonia, Santorini. It's a bit off the beaten path, but this local taverna is worth the trek. The food is rustic, hearty, and incredibly satisfying, with dishes like roasted lamb, stuffed peppers, and grilled octopus. The portions are generous, and the view of the island's landscape from the terrace is unbeatable.

4. Axiotissa (Naxos)

In Naxos, you'll want to stop by Axiotissa, a taverna that focuses on organic, farm-to-table dining. Naxos is known for its high-quality produce and dairy, and Axiotissa brings out the best in these ingredients. Expect dishes like slow-cooked goat, grilled vegetables, and fresh cheeses from the island's farms. It's a great spot for a relaxed, flavorful meal that showcases the best of Naxian cooking.

Rhodes: A Taste of History

Rhodes, one of Greece's largest islands, offers a unique blend of ancient history and vibrant food culture. The cuisine here reflects the island's strategic location as a meeting point between Europe and the East, so you'll find Greek staples with a touch of Middle Eastern influence.

1. Marco Polo Mansion (Rhodes Town)

Tucked away in the medieval streets of Rhodes Town, Marco Polo Mansion is a cozy, romantic spot where history meets fine dining. The menu combines traditional Greek flavors with a creative twist, offering dishes like lamb with yogurt sauce or octopus in a red wine reduction. The setting, in a beautifully restored old building, adds to the magic of the meal.

2. Hatzikelis (Rhodes Town)

For seafood lovers, Hatzikelis is one of the best places in Rhodes Town to enjoy fresh fish and other delights from the sea. Located near the harbor, this family-run taverna serves up grilled fish, shrimp saganaki, and octopus, all prepared simply to let the fresh flavors shine. The restaurant's location, close to the Medieval City, makes it a perfect stop after a day of exploring. The relaxed atmosphere and friendly service keep both locals and visitors coming back for more.

3. To Marouli (Rhodes Town)

For those looking for vegetarian or vegan options, To Marouli is a gem in the heart of Rhodes Town. This small, unpretentious restaurant offers a plant-based menu filled with vibrant, flavorful dishes like grilled veggies, salads bursting with local ingredients, and creative takes on traditional Greek recipes. The portions are generous, and the laid-back vibe makes it a perfect spot for a leisurely meal.

Corfu: A Blend of Greek and Italian Flavors

Corfu, located in the Ionian Sea, has a food culture that's distinct from the rest of Greece, thanks to the island's Venetian influences. The result is a unique fusion of Greek and Italian flavors that you won't find anywhere else.

1. Etrusco (Dassia, Corfu)

For an unforgettable dining experience, Etrusco is the place to go. Helmed by one of Greece's most renowned chefs, Ettore Botrini, this restaurant offers gourmet cuisine that beautifully blends Mediterranean flavors with modern techniques. The dishes are artfully presented, featuring seasonal ingredients from both Corfu and the mainland. From freshly caught seafood to creative pasta dishes, Etrusco is perfect for a special occasion or if you just want to treat yourself.

2. Taverna Tripa (Kinopiastes, Corfu)

For something more traditional, head to Taverna Tripa, one of the oldest and most famous tavernas in Corfu. Established in 1936, this taverna has been serving up rustic Greek food for generations. The menu is full of Corfiot classics like pastitsada (slow-cooked beef in tomato sauce with pasta), sofrito (veal cooked in white wine and garlic), and plenty of fresh, local wine. The portions are generous, and the atmosphere is lively, especially when the live music starts up.

3. Bougainvillea (Paleokastritsa, Corfu)

If you're after a meal with a view, Bougainvillea in Paleokastritsa is the perfect spot. Nestled on a hillside overlooking the sea, this taverna serves fresh, flavorful dishes made from local ingredients. Their seafood is especially good—try the grilled fish or the seafood pasta, which is packed with shrimp, mussels, and calamari. The views of the sunset over the Ionian Sea add an extra layer of magic to your meal.

The Peloponnese: Rustic and Authentic

The Peloponnese is often overlooked by travelers, but it's a foodie's paradise. The region's cuisine is hearty and rustic, drawing on local produce like olive oil, citrus, and wild greens. Here, you'll find some of the most authentic Greek food, prepared in traditional ways.

1. To Kati Allo (Nafplio)

If you're visiting the charming town of Nafplio, make sure to stop by To Kati Allo, a family-run taverna that's as cozy as it is delicious. The menu is full of home-cooked Greek favorites like gemista (stuffed tomatoes and peppers), kokkinisto (beef stew in tomato sauce), and grilled lamb. The friendly owners treat every guest like family, and the food is so good you'll want to return for seconds.

2. Kentrikon (Kardamyli)

In the picturesque village of Kardamyli, Kentrikon is the place to go for a taste of traditional Peloponnesian cooking. The dishes are simple yet bursting with flavor, with a focus on local ingredients like olive oil, honey, and herbs. Try the local lamb, slow-cooked with rosemary and lemon, or the horta (wild greens) sautéed with olive oil and lemon juice. The village atmosphere makes for a peaceful, authentic dining experience.

3. Telonio (Monemvasia)

Monemvasia is a beautiful fortified town, and Telonio offers an equally stunning dining experience. Set by the sea, the restaurant serves traditional Greek dishes with a modern twist. The seafood is especially good here— order the grilled octopus or the seafood orzo for a meal you won't forget. The restaurant also has an excellent wine list featuring local Peloponnesian wines.

Naxos: Where Farm-to-Table is the Norm

Naxos is known for its fertile land, making it one of the best places to enjoy fresh, local ingredients in Greece. The island produces some of the best cheese, potatoes, and olive oil in the country, and the food reflects that abundance.

1. Taverna Vassilis (Naxos Town)

For a traditional meal made with the freshest local ingredients, head to Taverna Vassilis. Located in Naxos Town, this family-run taverna offers hearty, home-cooked dishes that highlight the island's produce. Their stifado (a slow-cooked beef stew) and lamb baked with Naxian potatoes are especially popular. The portions are generous, and the service is always warm and friendly.

2. Axiotissa (Kastraki, Naxos)

We mentioned Axiotissa earlier, but it's worth a second mention here. This farm-to-table taverna is all about organic, local produce, and the menu changes daily depending on what's in season. Whether you're in the mood for grilled meats, fresh salads, or hearty vegetarian dishes, you'll find something delicious and packed with flavor. The relaxed setting and beautiful outdoor seating make it a perfect spot for a laid-back meal.

3. Scirocco (Naxos Town)

Another must-visit in Naxos Town is Scirocco, a beloved taverna known for its friendly service and comforting dishes. The menu features a mix of

Greek classics like moussaka and grilled meats, but also offers some creative twists on local recipes. It's the kind of place where you can sit back, relax, and enjoy a leisurely meal with a glass of local wine.

Best Places to Eat in a Jiffy

Athens

1. Varoulko Seaside

- **Address:** Akti Koumoundourou 52, Mikrolimano, Piraeus
- **Opening Hours:** Daily 13:00 – 00:00
- **Price Range:** €50 – €100 per person

2. Oineas Restaurant

- **Address:** Esopou 9, Psiri, Athens
- **Opening Hours:** Daily 12:00 – 00:00
- **Price Range:** €20 – €40 per person

3. Avli

- **Address:** Agiou Dimitriou 12, Psirri, Athens
- **Opening Hours:** Daily 13:00 – 00:00
- **Price Range:** €15 – €30 per person

4. Ta Karamanlidika Tou Fani

- **Address:** Sokratous 1, Psiri, Athens
- **Opening Hours:** Monday – Saturday 12:00 – 23:30
- **Price Range:** €10 – €25 per person

Thessaloniki

1. Mourga

- **Address:** Ionos Dragoumi 6, Thessaloniki
- **Opening Hours:** Tuesday – Saturday 13:00 – 23:00
- **Price Range:** €15 – €35 per person

2. Extravaganza

- **Address:** Ptolemeon 29A, Thessaloniki
- **Opening Hours:** Tuesday – Sunday 12:00 – 23:00
- **Price Range:** €15 – €30 per person

3. Sempriko

- **Address:** Frangon 2, Thessaloniki
- **Opening Hours:** Monday – Saturday 13:00 – 00:00
- **Price Range:** €20 – €40 per person

Crete

1. Peskesi

- **Address:** Kapetan Haralampi 6-8, Heraklion
- **Opening Hours:** Daily 12:00 – 00:00
- **Price Range:** €20 – €40 per person

2. Tamam

- **Address:** Zambeliou 49, Chania
- **Opening Hours:** Daily 12:00 – 23:30
- **Price Range:** €15 – €35 per person

3. Thalassino Ageri

- **Address:** Vivilaki 35, Chania
- **Opening Hours:** Daily 13:00 – 23:00
- **Price Range:** €25 – €45 per person

The Cyclades

1. Selene

- **Address:** Fira, Santorini
- **Opening Hours:** Daily 18:30 – 23:00
- **Price Range:** €60 – €120 per person

2. Kiki's Tavern

- **Address:** Agios Sostis Beach, Mykonos
- **Opening Hours:** Daily 12:00 – 19:00 (no reservations)
- **Price Range:** €20 – €35 per person

3. Metaxi Mas

- **Address:** Exo Gonia, Santorini
- **Opening Hours:** Daily 13:00 – 23:00
- **Price Range:** €25 – €40 per person

4. Axiotissa

- **Address:** Kastraki Beach, Naxos
- **Opening Hours:** Daily 13:00 – 23:00

- **Price Range:** €15 – €30 per person

Rhodes
1. Marco Polo Mansion
- **Address:** Agiou Fanouriou 40, Old Town, Rhodes
- **Opening Hours:** Monday – Saturday 19:00 – 23:30
- **Price Range:** €30 – €60 per person

2. Hatzikelis
- **Address:** Sofokleous 24, Old Town, Rhodes
- **Opening Hours:** Daily 12:00 – 23:00
- **Price Range:** €20 – €40 per person

3. To Marouli
- **Address:** Platonos 26, Old Town, Rhodes
- **Opening Hours:** Monday – Saturday 12:00 – 23:00
- **Price Range:** €10 – €25 per person

Corfu
1. Etrusco
- **Address:** Kato Korakiana, Dassia, Corfu
- **Opening Hours:** Tuesday – Sunday 19:00 – 23:00
- **Price Range:** €60 – €120 per person

2. Taverna Tripa
- **Address:** Kinopiastes, Corfu
- **Opening Hours:** Daily 13:00 – 23:00
- **Price Range:** €20 – €40 per person

3. Bougainvillea
- **Address:** Paleokastritsa, Corfu
- **Opening Hours:** Daily 12:00 – 22:00
- **Price Range:** €15 – €30 per person

The Peloponnese
1. To Kati Allo
- **Address:** 16 Staikopoulou St, Nafplio
- **Opening Hours:** Daily 12:00 – 23:00
- **Price Range:** €10 – €20 per person

2. Kentrikon
- **Address:** Main Square, Kardamyli
- **Opening Hours:** Daily 13:00 – 22:00
- **Price Range:** €15 – €30 per person

3. Telonio
- **Address:** Kato Poli, Monemvasia
- **Opening Hours:** Daily 13:00 – 23:00
- **Price Range:** €25 – €45 per person

Naxos

1. Taverna Vassilis

- **Address:** Naxos Town, Naxos

- **Opening Hours:** Daily 12:00 – 23:00

- **Price Range:** €15 – €30 per person

2. Axiotissa

- **Address:** Kastraki, Naxos

- **Opening Hours:** Daily 13:00 – 23:00

- **Price Range:** €15 – €30 per person

3. Scirocco

- **Address:** Protopapadaki St., Naxos Town, Naxos

- **Opening Hours:** Daily 12:00 – 23:30

- **Price Range:** €10 – €25 per person

Chapter Seven

Local Etiquettes, Customs, and Interactions in Greece

W hen you visit Greece, you'll quickly notice that it's a country where culture and tradition run deep. Greek people are known for their warmth, generosity, and genuine hospitality. Understanding a few local customs and social norms will not only help you blend in but also allow you to connect more meaningfully with the locals. Whether you're sitting down for a meal, wandering through a village, or attending a festival, a little awareness of the way things work here can go a long way.

Greek Hospitality: "PHILOXENIA" – The Love of Strangers

One of the most important concepts in Greek culture is philoxenia, which literally means "friend to strangers." Greeks take hospitality seriously, and you'll experience this firsthand as soon as you arrive. Locals are incredibly warm and welcoming to visitors, often going out of their way to make sure you feel comfortable.

If you're invited to a Greek home, consider it an honor. Don't be surprised if they offer you coffee, a drink, or something to eat—philoxenia is all about making guests feel at home. It's polite to accept their hospitality, even if it's just a small snack or drink. It's also common for Greeks to insist on offering more food or drink, so don't hesitate to politely decline if you've had enough—though they may encourage you to have more!

A small gift is always appreciated if you're visiting someone's home. Bringing sweets, wine, or flowers is a nice gesture to show your appreciation. Greeks love giving and receiving gifts, and even something simple will be met with gratitude.

Greetings and Social Interactions

Greeks are generally very friendly and open, and they love to engage in conversation. When greeting someone, it's common to say **yassou (hello)** in informal settings, or **yassas** if you're addressing a group or someone older. You'll also hear **kalimera (good morning), kalispera (good evening)**, and **kalinychta (good night)** frequently throughout the day.

A handshake is the standard way to greet someone you're meeting for the first time. Among friends and family, it's common to exchange kisses on both cheeks, starting with the right cheek. If you're not sure how familiar you are with someone, wait for them to make the first move.

Greeks also tend to stand close when speaking and are not afraid of physical contact. They may place a hand on your shoulder or arm during conversation, which is a sign of friendliness. Don't be alarmed by this closeness; it's part of the culture.

Time in Greece: Take It Slow

One of the first things you'll notice about Greece is the relaxed attitude toward time. The pace of life is slow, especially in the islands and rural areas. While people are punctual for formal events like business meetings or appointments, in everyday life, things tend to happen a little later than planned.

Meals, for instance, are often leisurely affairs, especially dinner, which is typically eaten late, around 8 or 9 p.m. It's common to linger at the table for hours, enjoying conversation, food, and drinks. Don't feel rushed— take your time and enjoy the experience.

If you're meeting someone for coffee or a casual get-together, don't be surprised if they arrive 10-15 minutes late. In Greece, this isn't seen as rude; it's just the way things are. However, it's always a good idea to be punctual yourself, especially for formal events or when meeting someone for the first time.

Dining Etiquette

Eating in Greece is a communal experience, and there's a lot of emphasis on sharing food. Whether you're at a restaurant or a family gathering, dishes are often placed in the center of the table for everyone to share. It's all about trying a bit of everything and enjoying the variety of flavors. Here are a few tips to keep in mind when dining in Greece:

Table Manners: Wait for your host to start eating before you dig in. It's customary for the host to invite everyone to start the meal by saying **kali orexi (bon appétit)**. If you're the guest, don't be surprised if the host tries to serve you first or offers to put food on your plate.

Sharing Food: Don't hesitate to try everything on the table. Greeks love when guests enjoy the food, and they may encourage you to have second helpings. It's polite to try a little bit of everything, even if you're not too familiar with the dishes.

Bread and Olive Oil: In Greece, bread is often served with meals, and it's common to dip it in olive oil. Don't hesitate to break off a piece of bread and use it to mop up sauces or olive oil—this is perfectly acceptable.

Drinks: If you're drinking alcohol, you'll notice that Greeks often make a toast before the first sip, saying **stin ygeia mas (to our health)**. It's considered polite to join in. Water is always served with meals, and Greeks often drink it alongside wine or ouzo.

When you're finished with your meal, placing your fork and knife parallel on your plate signals that you're done. Tipping is appreciated but not mandatory. If you do decide to leave a tip, around 5-10% is considered generous in Greece.

Coffee Culture

Greeks take their coffee seriously. Whether you're grabbing a quick frappe (iced coffee) or sitting down for a leisurely cup of Greek coffee, you'll notice that coffee is more than just a drink here—it's a ritual. Greeks love to sit at cafés and chat for hours over coffee, so don't be surprised if your quick coffee break turns into a long, relaxed experience.

Greek coffee is thick, strong, and served in small cups. It's similar to Turkish coffee, and it's brewed slowly in a small pot called a briki. The grounds settle at the bottom, so don't drink all the way to the bottom of the cup unless you enjoy a mouthful of grit!

If you're ordering a coffee, you'll need to specify how sweet you like it. There are three basic levels of sweetness for Greek coffee:

- Sketos (no sugar)
- Metrios (medium sweetness)
- Glykos (very sweet)

For cold coffee lovers, frappe is a popular choice in the summer. It's made with instant coffee, sugar, and milk, all shaken together and served over ice. You can also try a freddo espresso or freddo cappuccino, both of which are cold versions of their Italian counterparts.

Respect for Religion and Traditions

Greece is a predominantly Orthodox Christian country, and religion plays a significant role in daily life. You'll see churches everywhere, from tiny chapels in the mountains to grand cathedrals in the cities. While Greeks are generally open and accepting, it's important to be respectful when visiting religious sites.

If you're planning to visit a church or monastery, be mindful of your clothing. Men and women are expected to dress modestly, with shoulders and knees covered. In some monasteries, women may also be required to wear long skirts, but these are often provided at the entrance.

During religious holidays, especially Easter, the atmosphere in Greece becomes deeply spiritual. Easter is the most important holiday in Greece, and many traditions, such as the midnight church service and the Easter feast, are observed across the country. If you happen to be in Greece during Easter, it's a wonderful opportunity to witness these customs firsthand, but remember to approach them with respect.

Greek Superstitions and Gestures

Greeks are a superstitious bunch, and you might come across a few traditions or gestures that seem unusual if you're not familiar with them.

The Mati (Evil Eye): One of the most common superstitions in Greece is the belief in the mati, or evil eye. Many Greeks believe that a person can cast the evil eye unintentionally through jealousy or envy, causing bad luck or illness. You'll often see people wearing a blue eye charm to ward off the evil eye. If someone compliments you, they may add, "na mi se matiaso" (may I not give you the evil eye) as a form of protection.

Hand Gestures: Greeks are expressive speakers and use a lot of hand gestures, but there are a few you should avoid. For example, holding your hand out, palm facing forward, is seen as an offensive gesture. This gesture, known as the moutza, is the equivalent of showing someone your middle finger. Be mindful of how you use your hands during conversations, and when in doubt, keep your palms facing inward.

Public Behavior and Social Norms

Greeks are generally easygoing, but there are a few social norms to be aware of when interacting in public spaces.

Noise Levels: Greeks tend to speak loudly and passionately, especially when they're excited or engaged in conversation. Don't mistake this for anger—it's just part of the culture. You'll often hear people debating politics or discussing their favorite soccer team with great enthusiasm.

Queuing: In some parts of Greece, especially in rural areas, the concept of waiting in line is a bit more relaxed. People may not always form an orderly queue, especially in busy places like bakeries or markets. If you notice someone getting served ahead of you, don't take it personally—it's all part of the local rhythm.

Smoking: Smoking is still quite common in Greece, and you'll find that many locals enjoy a cigarette, even in public places like cafés or bars. While there are regulations against indoor smoking, enforcement can be lax in some areas, especially in smaller establishments. If you're a non-smoker, it's always a good idea to politely ask if smoking is allowed when you're sitting indoors. Outdoors, it's more accepted, and you'll often see people smoking while having coffee or drinks at a café.

Personal Space and Conversations

Greeks are naturally warm and open, which sometimes means they might get a little closer than you're used to during conversations. Personal space is more flexible in Greece, especially among friends and family, so don't be surprised if someone stands close or touches your arm while speaking to you. This physical closeness is a sign of friendliness and engagement, not intrusion.

Conversations in Greece tend to be lively and full of expression. People may speak passionately about a topic, using hand gestures and raising their voices, especially when discussing something like politics, sports, or food. This isn't aggression; it's just part of how Greeks communicate. They love a good debate and don't shy away from discussing big topics, even with strangers.

At the same time, be mindful of the context. While Greeks are open to many discussions, topics like personal wealth, religion, or very private matters are generally avoided unless you know someone well. It's better to focus on universal topics like travel, family, or food when engaging in light conversation.

Greek Festivals: Joining the Celebration

If there's one thing Greeks love, it's a good celebration. Festivals, or panigyria, are a huge part of Greek life, and they're held throughout the year in honor of saints, religious holidays, or local traditions. These festivals often involve live music, dancing, and—of course—lots of food.

Participating in a Festival: If you find yourself in Greece during one of these events, you're in for a treat. Everyone is welcome, and it's common for locals to invite visitors to join in the celebrations. Don't hesitate to participate, whether it's dancing to traditional Greek music, enjoying the feast, or simply soaking in the lively atmosphere.

The most important festival in Greece is **Easter**, celebrated with special church services, family gatherings, and a grand feast. It's a time of joy and renewal, and if you're lucky enough to be invited to an Easter meal, be prepared for lamb on the spit, red-dyed eggs, and lots of traditional sweets. Greeks often greet each other during this time with Christos Anesti (Christ is risen), to which the response is Alithos Anesti (truly, He is risen).

Another big celebration is **name days,** which are like a second birthday for many Greeks. Instead of celebrating the date of their birth, many people celebrate on the day of the saint they are named after. On these occasions, the person whose name day it is often hosts friends and family for food and drinks. It's not expected for the guests to bring gifts, but a small gesture like flowers or sweets is always appreciated.

Tipping and Paying the Bill

In Greece, tipping isn't mandatory, but it's always appreciated. If you're happy with the service, a small tip goes a long way in showing your gratitude. Here's a quick guide to tipping etiquette in different situations:

Restaurants: In most casual places, rounding up the bill or leaving an extra €1-€5 is sufficient. In higher-end restaurants, leaving a tip of 5-10% of the total bill is considered generous. The server may not bring the bill until you ask for it, as it's customary to take your time and enjoy your meal without being rushed.

Cafés and Bars: At a café or bar, it's common to leave a small tip—usually the change from your bill or €1-€2, depending on the size of the order.

Taxis: For taxi drivers, rounding up the fare is common. If the driver has been especially helpful or friendly, you can leave a little extra, but there's no pressure to tip large amounts.

Hotels: For hotel staff like porters or housekeepers, it's polite to leave a small tip (€1-€2) for each service. If you've received exceptional service, a little extra goes a long way to show your appreciation.

Embracing the Greek Way of Life

At the heart of Greece's customs and etiquette is a deep sense of connection, community, and shared experiences. Greeks live by the philosophy that life is to be enjoyed, and they take time to savor moments, whether that's over a meal, during a conversation, or while celebrating a festival.

As a traveler, embracing this laid-back, friendly approach will make your experience even richer. Don't rush through your meals; linger at the table, chat with locals, and take in the sights and sounds around you. When someone invites you into their world, whether it's a conversation at a café or a meal at their home, it's an invitation to become part of their community, even if only for a short time.

Simple Local Interactions: Common Phrases and Their Meaning

Everyday Greetings

Yassou (Γεια σου) – Hello (informal)

This is the most common way to say "hello" in Greece, especially when you're speaking to someone you know, or when you're in an informal setting. It's friendly and casual, perfect for everyday interactions.

Yassas (Γεια σας) – Hello (formal/plural)

If you're greeting a group of people or speaking to someone older or in a more formal situation, use yassas. It's the more polite version of "hello," and it can also mean "goodbye" when you're parting ways.

Kalimera (Καλημέρα) – Good morning

You'll hear this a lot in the morning, as it's the go-to greeting until around noon. It's a warm and welcoming way to start your day, whether you're greeting someone at a café or just passing by.

Kalispera (Καλησπέρα) – Good afternoon/evening

From midday onward, switch to kalispera. It's perfect when you're meeting someone in the late afternoon or early evening. It's a polite and friendly way to acknowledge the time of day.

Kalinychta (Καληνύχτα) – Good night

When you're heading to bed or leaving someone in the evening, kalinychta is what you'll want to say. It's a gentle way to wish someone a good night's rest.

Polite Expressions

Efharisto (Ευχαριστώ) – Thank you

Learning how to say "thank you" in Greek is essential. Whether you've received directions or been served a meal, saying efharisto goes a long way. The locals appreciate the effort, and it's a simple way to show gratitude.

Parakalo (Παρακαλώ) – You're welcome / Please

Parakalo is one of the most versatile words in Greek. Not only does it mean "you're welcome" when someone thanks you, but it can also be used to say "please." You'll often hear it when someone is offering you something or when they're asking for something politely.

Signomi (Συγγνώμη) – Excuse me / I'm sorry

If you bump into someone, need to get someone's attention, or want to apologize for something, signomi is your go-to phrase. It's polite and shows respect for the other person's space or time.

Me sigchorite (Με συγχωρείτε) – Pardon me / Sorry (more formal)

A slightly more formal way of saying "excuse me" or "sorry" is me sigchorite. Use this when you're in a more formal setting or if you want to show extra politeness.

Asking for Help or Directions

Pou ine...? (Πού είναι...?) – Where is...?

Whether you're looking for the nearest beach, a bathroom, or a specific landmark, pou ine is what you'll need to ask for directions. Just follow it up with the place you're trying to find.

Example:

Pou ine i paralia? (Πού είναι η παραλία?) – Where is the beach?

Pos na pao sto…? (Πώς να πάω στο...?) – How do I get to…?

If you're trying to find out how to reach a certain place, this is the phrase to use. It's especially helpful if you're navigating a city or town on foot or by public transport.

Example:
Pos na pao sto Plaka? (Πώς να πάω στο Πλάκα?) – How do I get to Plaka?

Borite na me voithisete? (Μπορείτε να με βοηθήσετε?) – Can you help me?

If you're lost or just need some assistance, this is a polite way to ask for help. Greeks are generally helpful and friendly, and this phrase will show that you're asking kindly.

Ti ora ine? (Τι ώρα είναι?) – What time is it?

When you need to check the time but don't have your phone handy, you can ask someone nearby ti ora ine. It's a simple and useful phrase to know when you're trying to catch a bus or make it to a reservation on time.

In a Café or Restaurant

Thelo… (Θέλω…) – I want…

When ordering food or drinks, start your sentence with thelo, which means "I want." It's a straightforward and polite way to order something.

163

Example:

Thelo ena kafe, parakalo (Θέλω έναν καφέ, παρακαλώ) – I want a coffee, please.

Ena kafe, parakalo (Ένα καφέ, παρακαλώ) – One coffee, please

A quick way to order a coffee in Greece. Coffee culture is huge here, so whether you want a traditional Greek coffee or a cold frappe, this phrase will come in handy.

To logariasmo, parakalo (Τον λογαριασμό, παρακαλώ) – The bill, please

When you're ready to settle up, this is the phrase you'll use to ask for the bill. In Greece, it's common for the waiter to wait until you ask for the bill rather than bringing it automatically, so don't hesitate to use this phrase when you're ready to leave.

Exete orexi? (Έχετε όρεξη?) – Do you have an appetite?

If someone asks you this, they're inviting you to enjoy a meal or snack. Food is a big part of Greek hospitality, and it's common to hear this phrase at gatherings. A simple way to respond is, Nai, efharisto! (Yes, thank you!).

Ti ine afto? (Τι είναι αυτό;) – What is this?

If you're not sure what a dish is or you're curious about a local specialty, this phrase is your friend. Greeks love to talk about their food, so asking ti ine afto might even lead to some recommendations!

Shopping and Money

Poso kanei? (Πόσο κάνει;) – How much does it cost?

When shopping in markets, boutiques, or even at small souvenir stands, poso kanei will help you ask for the price of something. It's a key phrase when you're out and about looking for gifts or local goods.

Ine polu akrivo! (Είναι πολύ ακριβό!) – It's too expensive!

If something is a bit out of your budget, don't be shy to say ine polu akrivo. In some places, you might be able to negotiate a better price, especially in local markets.

Me poso? (Με πόσο;) – For how much?

If you're bargaining or negotiating, this is a shorter way of asking for the price. It's helpful in places like flea markets or when buying handmade crafts from local vendors.

Tha to paro (Θα το πάρω) – I'll take it

When you've made your choice and you're ready to buy something, this is the phrase you'll need. It's quick and easy, letting the seller know you're ready to make the purchase.

Essential Travel Phrases

Endaxi (Εντάξει) – Okay / All right

You'll hear this word everywhere in Greece, and it's used in all kinds of situations. Whether you're agreeing to something, confirming an order, or just acknowledging what someone said, endaxi is a casual, catch-all phrase that you'll get used to quickly.

Pou ine i toualeta? (Πού είναι η τουαλέτα;) – Where is the toilet?

This is a vital phrase to know when you're out and about, especially if you're in a café, restaurant, or public space. Locals will be happy to point you in the right direction.

Dhen katalaveno (Δεν καταλαβαίνω) – I don't understand

If you're having trouble understanding something, use this phrase. Most Greeks will try to switch to English if they see you're struggling with the language, but it's polite to let them know you didn't quite catch what they were saying.

Milate Anglika? (Μιλάτε Αγγλικά;) – Do you speak English?

This is an important question when you're stuck and need help in English. Many Greeks speak English, especially in tourist areas, but it's always nice to ask politely. If they do, they'll switch over, but even if they don't, they'll often do their best to assist you.

Pou einai to aerodromio? (Πού είναι το αεροδρόμιο?) – Where is the airport?
When you're ready to catch a flight or need directions to the nearest airport, this phrase is a helpful way to ask for assistance.

Numbers and Time

Ena (Ένα) – One
Dyo (Δύο) – Two
Tria (Τρία) – Three
Tessera (Τέσσερα) – Four
Pente (Πέντε) – Five

Learning numbers in Greek can be really handy, especially when shopping or ordering multiple items. Numbers help you specify how many things you want or need.

Ti ora einai? (Τι ώρα είναι?) – What time is it?
If you need to know the time, this phrase will help. It's especially useful if you're waiting for a bus or need to catch a ferry.

Expressing Yourself

Mou aresi (Μου αρέσει) – I like it

Whether you're complimenting the food, enjoying a view, or appreciating a souvenir, this is a great way to express your approval. Saying mou aresi is always a good way to connect with locals when they ask how you're enjoying something.

Ise poli omorfos/omorfi (Είσαι πολύ όμορφος/όμορφη) – You are very handsome/beautiful

If you want to compliment someone's appearance, use this phrase. Omorfos is for a man, and omorfi is for a woman. It's a nice way to give a sincere compliment in Greek.

Ti kaneis? (Τι κάνεις?) – How are you?

This is a friendly greeting when you meet someone, and it's a great way to start a conversation. You can follow it up with ola kala? (All good?) to keep things casual.

Eimai kala (Είμαι καλά) – I'm fine

If someone asks how you are, this is a simple way to respond. If you're feeling really good, you can say eimai poly kala (I'm very well).

Farewells

Antio (Αντίο) – Goodbye

A simple way to say goodbye, antio is used when you're parting ways, whether it's with a friend, a store clerk, or a hotel receptionist.

Tha ta poume (Θα τα πούμε) – See you later

If you plan to see someone again, tha ta poume is a more casual and friendly way of saying "goodbye." It's great when you're planning to meet up with someone later or soon.

Kalo taxidi (Καλό ταξίδι) – Have a good trip

If someone is traveling, this is a nice way to wish them a safe and enjoyable journey. It's a thoughtful farewell, often used when someone is heading out of town or leaving for the airport.

Chapter Eight

Itinerary, Flights, and Getting Around

Planning your dream trip to Greece? You're in for a treat! This Mediterranean paradise isn't just about postcard-perfect beaches and ancient ruins – it's also a land where the laid-back vibe of the islands meets the cultural buzz of historic cities. Whether you're staying a week or a month, there's plenty to see and do. Let's talk about how to map out your trip, catch the right flight, and get around this beautiful country without a hitch.

Crafting the Perfect Itinerary: Greece, Your Way

One of the best things about Greece is its variety. Whether you're all about exploring ancient ruins, wandering through charming villages, hiking mountains, or lounging on a beach with a cold drink, Greece has something for you. But with so much to do, where should you start?

Start in Athens, of course

Your Greek adventure will likely kick off in Athens, the capital and heart of the country. With direct flights from most major cities worldwide, Athens is the easiest place to begin. Spend at least two or three days here to soak up the history, starting with the Acropolis. But don't just stick to the tourist spots—take a walk through Plaka, the oldest neighborhood, and explore its narrow, winding streets lined with cozy cafés and artisan shops. You'll get a real taste of Athenian life.

Pro tip: Be sure to visit the Acropolis Museum. It's just as impressive as the ruins themselves, and the view from its café will give you a fresh perspective on the city. After a couple of days, it's time to hit the road – or ferry!

The Cyclades: Island hopping at its finest

After you've explored Athens, it's time to head to the islands. The Cyclades are the most popular group of islands and for good reason. Picture this: whitewashed buildings, blue-domed churches, crystal-clear water, and sunsets that will leave you speechless.

Santorini is the showstopper here. Famous for its breathtaking views and romance, it's the perfect place to unwind. But, don't just park yourself at a luxury hotel! Rent a scooter and explore smaller towns like Pyrgos or Megalochori. They're quieter, but just as beautiful.

Mykonos is another popular stop, especially if you're in the mood to party. Beyond its bustling nightlife, Mykonos has charming villages and hidden beaches that are worth discovering. Try heading to Agios Sostis Beach for some peace and quiet – it's a local favorite.

If you have extra time, add Naxos or Paros to your itinerary. These islands are just a short ferry ride from their more famous neighbors, but they offer a slower pace of life and fewer crowds, making them perfect for exploring traditional Greek culture.

Crete: A whole other world

The biggest of the Greek islands, Crete deserves at least a few days on your itinerary. It's a place that feels like a country in itself, with mountains, ancient Minoan ruins, and beaches that stretch for miles. Start in Chania, a city on the northwest coast known for its Venetian harbor and vibrant markets. Then, if you're up for some hiking, head to the Samaria Gorge for a trek through one of Europe's longest canyons.

And don't miss Elafonisi Beach – the water here is so clear and shallow, you'll feel like you're walking on air. Plus, the sand has a pinkish hue that's straight out of a dream.

Flights: Getting to Greece and Beyond

Now that you've got a rough idea of where to go, let's talk logistics – specifically, how to get to Greece. Luckily, flying to Greece has never been easier, with direct flights from many international hubs.

International Flights

For most travelers, **Athens International Airport (Eleftherios Venizelos)** is your gateway into the country. It's a major hub, and direct flights from cities like New York, London, Paris, and Dubai make getting here a breeze. Several budget airlines also serve Athens, so if you're coming from Europe, you can snag some pretty affordable fares.

But Athens isn't your only option. Depending on your itinerary, you could also fly into Thessaloniki, Greece's second-largest city in the north, or even directly to Heraklion or Chania if Crete is your first stop. These airports handle several international flights during the summer months, though they're smaller than Athens.

Pro tip: If you're looking to save some cash, check for flights to other European cities and then book a low-cost flight to Greece separately. It might take a little extra time, but sometimes the savings are worth it!

Domestic Flights: Island Hopping from the Sky

Once you've landed in Greece, you've got a couple of options for getting to the islands. While ferries are the classic way to travel, Greece has an extensive domestic flight network that can save you time.

Several airlines operate domestic routes between Athens and the islands, including **Aegean Airlines, Sky Express, and Ryanair**. These short flights (usually 30 to 60 minutes) will whisk you away to islands like

Santorini, Mykonos, Crete, and Rhodes, cutting down travel time significantly if you're on a tight schedule.

Pro tip: Domestic flights can fill up fast during the summer months, so it's worth booking ahead if you're traveling in peak season. And keep in mind that some islands, especially the smaller ones, don't have airports, so ferries will be your best bet.

Ferries: Slow Down and Sail

No trip to Greece is complete without a ferry ride. Whether you're cruising from Athens to the Cyclades or island-hopping within a group, ferries are part of the experience. Plus, you get to enjoy the stunning views of the Aegean Sea along the way.

Types of Ferries

There are two main types of ferries: **high-speed and regular ferries**. High-speed ferries (run by companies like Seajets or Hellenic Seaways) will get you from Athens to Santorini in around 4 to 5 hours, while the regular ferries take closer to 8 hours. High-speed options are pricier, but you'll save time – and trust me, time is precious when you're on vacation!

That said, the regular ferries have a charm of their own. They're larger, with outdoor decks where you can soak up the sun and enjoy the sea breeze. If you're not in a rush and like the idea of a more leisurely pace, this is the way to go. You might even meet some locals who'll share insider tips or just chat about life on the islands.

Booking Your Ferry Tickets
While you can buy ferry tickets at the port, it's a good idea to book ahead, especially during the busy summer season. Online platforms like FerryHopper make it easy to compare prices and schedules for different routes, and most ferries run regularly during peak months (May to September). Outside of that window, the ferry schedules can be less frequent, so plan accordingly.

Pro tip: Greek ferries are known for delays, so if you're catching a flight or have a tight schedule, plan for a little cushion time.

Getting Around Greece

Now that you've arrived, let's talk about how to actually get around the mainland and the islands.

Mainland Travel
On the mainland, renting a car is one of the best ways to explore Greece. The major cities like Athens and Thessaloniki have reliable public transportation, but if you want to venture into the countryside – think the monasteries of Meteora, the ancient ruins of Delphi, or the rugged terrain of the Peloponnese – you'll want your own wheels. Just remember, Greek

roads can be narrow and winding, especially in rural areas. So, take your time and enjoy the journey!

Pro tip: If you're driving in Greece, be prepared for tolls on some highways, and always make sure you have cash on hand for smaller roads where cards might not be accepted.

Getting Around the Islands

Once you're on the islands, you've got a few options. If you're sticking to bigger towns, walking is often the best way to go. Places like Mykonos Town or Fira in Santorini are best explored on foot, and trying to drive through the tiny, cobblestone streets would be a headache anyway.

For longer distances, consider renting a scooter or ATV – it's an affordable and fun way to zip around the islands. Just make sure you're comfortable driving, as some roads can be steep or gravelly, especially if you're exploring more remote areas.

For those who prefer not to drive, buses run regularly between the major towns and beaches on most islands. They're cheap, reliable, and a good way to see the local way of life. Taxis are another option, though they can get pricey, especially on the more touristy islands.

Flights: Into Greece and Out of Greece

Flying to Greece is your first big step into a journey of sun-soaked islands, ancient ruins, and incredible food. Whether you're coming from the other side of the world or hopping over from a nearby European country, flying into Greece is easier than you might think. And when it's time to leave, the same rule applies—catching a flight out of Greece is just as straightforward. Let's break it down so you know what to expect and how to make your travels as smooth as possible.

Getting into Greece: Welcome to the Heart of the Mediterranean

Most international travelers will land in Athens, but Greece has a few other airports worth considering, depending on your plans. If you're coming from the U.S., Canada, or Asia, Athens is going to be your gateway. But don't worry, even if your ultimate destination is an island or somewhere up north, it's easy to connect to your next stop.

Athens International Airport (Eleftherios Venizelos)

Athens International Airport is the main entry point for visitors from around the world. This modern and well-organized airport is located about 35 kilometers (22 miles) outside the city center, so it's not far at all from the action. You can grab a taxi, hop on a bus, or take the metro directly from the airport into Athens.

The best part? Athens is well-connected to major cities across the globe. Whether you're flying from New York, London, Dubai, or Sydney, you'll likely find direct or one-stop flights throughout the year. Airlines like Aegean, Olympic Air, Emirates, and several low-cost carriers serve Athens. If you're lucky, you might even snag a great deal if you book early or keep an eye out for those flash sales.

If you're coming from within Europe, things get even better. There are plenty of budget airlines, like Ryanair and EasyJet, which offer cheap flights to Athens from cities across Europe. So, if you're starting your trip elsewhere in Europe, you can easily find a flight that won't break the bank.

Pro tip: Athens International Airport also makes for a great hub if you're planning on exploring the islands or other parts of Greece. You can hop on a domestic flight or catch a ferry without too much hassle.

Other Entry Points: Thessaloniki and the Islands
While Athens is the go-to for most travelers, there are other options if you're planning a more tailored trip.

Thessaloniki: If your itinerary takes you north, look into flights to Thessaloniki. It's Greece's second-largest city, and it's got its own international airport **(Makedonia Airport)**. This is perfect if you're headed toward the beautiful beaches of **Halkidiki** or exploring northern Greece. You'll find direct flights here from many European cities, but fewer options from outside the continent.

The Islands: Some of Greece's larger islands have international airports too, which can be a lifesaver if you're aiming to skip mainland Greece altogether. Islands like Santorini, Mykonos, Rhodes, Crete, and Corfu offer direct flights from other European cities, especially during the summer months. During high season, many airlines ramp up their service to these sun-drenched islands, making it easy to fly directly without needing to stop in Athens.

For example, if you're planning a romantic getaway to Santorini or a wild adventure in Mykonos, you might be able to fly directly to these islands from major hubs like London, Paris, or Berlin. No ferry necessary!

Timing Your Arrival

When it comes to flying into Greece, timing is everything. Peak tourist season in Greece runs from June to September, so flights during this period can be more expensive and busier. If you're planning a summer getaway, aim to book your flights a few months in advance to lock in better prices.

If you're lucky enough to travel in the off-season (April to May or October to November), you'll find more affordable flights and fewer crowds. While some of the islands might be quieter, this is the perfect time to experience a more laid-back version of Greece. Plus, the weather is still pretty great!

Domestic Flights: Island-Hopping Made Easy

Once you've landed in Greece, you might be itching to get to the islands or another part of the country. While ferries are the traditional way to travel between the islands, domestic flights are an excellent option if you're short on time.

Athens International Airport is a hub for domestic flights, so it's a breeze to catch a short flight to places like Crete, Rhodes, or Corfu. Domestic flights are quick, usually lasting between 30 minutes and an hour, making it possible to start your island adventures in no time. Airlines like Aegean Airlines, Olympic Air, and Sky Express serve these routes, often with multiple flights a day, especially in the summer.

Pro tip: Domestic flights can be a great time-saver if you're island-hopping. Instead of spending hours on a ferry, you can fly from Athens to Santorini or Mykonos in about 45 minutes. Plus, domestic flights are often very affordable if you book early, so keep an eye out for deals.

Leaving Greece: All Good Things Must Come to an End

When it's time to leave Greece (and trust me, you won't want to), you've got a few options. Just like getting in, Athens is going to be your main gateway for flights out of the country. Most major airlines offer flights back to their hubs, and connections to other European cities are a breeze.

If you're flying to another European country, direct flights are common and plentiful. From there, you can easily connect to just about any part of the world. Alternatively, if your trip includes more than just Greece, consider flying from one of the islands to your next destination. This way, you don't have to backtrack to Athens.

Preparing for Your Departure

Leaving Greece is straightforward, but there are a few things to keep in mind to make your departure smooth. If you're flying out of Athens International Airport, aim to arrive a couple of hours before your flight. While the airport is modern and efficient, security lines can get long, especially during the busy summer months. Fortunately, there are plenty of shops and restaurants to keep you entertained if you have some time to kill.

If you're flying out from one of the smaller islands, keep in mind that island airports are, well, small. Expect minimal facilities and plan to arrive early, as flights can sometimes be delayed due to wind or weather.

Pro tip: If you're departing on an international flight, remember that you might have to go through passport control, which can add a bit of extra time. Always check your airline's recommendations on when to arrive at the airport.

Final Leg: Connecting Flights

If your flight out of Greece isn't direct and you've got a layover in another European city, the good news is that most European airports are well-connected. Whether you're passing through Rome, Munich, or London, layovers tend to be smooth and efficient.

Just make sure to keep an eye on your baggage allowance, especially if you're switching from a low-cost airline to a full-service carrier. What might be free on one airline could cost you extra on another, so double-check before you pack those extra souvenirs!

Tips for Getting Around: Visa Requirements

Before you start daydreaming about your Greek getaway, let's talk about something practical: visas. We know, we know, it's not the most exciting topic. But getting your visa situation sorted is one of those things you'll be glad you took care of early. Luckily, for most visitors, Greece is pretty straightforward when it comes to entry requirements. Whether you need a visa or not largely depends on where you're from, how long you're planning to stay, and what your travel goals are. Let's break it all down, nice and easy.

Do You Need a Visa to Visit Greece?

The answer to this question really depends on where you're from. But for many travelers, visiting Greece for a short stay is a breeze. If you're planning on staying less than 90 days and you're coming from a country with visa-free access, you won't need a visa at all. Greece is part of the

Schengen Area, which is a group of 27 European countries that have agreed to a common visa policy. This means that a visa for Greece works the same as a visa for any other Schengen country.

Travelers from the EU/EEA and Switzerland

If you're a citizen of an EU or EEA country, or Switzerland, you're in luck! No visa is required for you. You can travel freely into Greece, and there are no time limits for how long you can stay. All you need is a valid passport or ID card, and you're good to go.

For EU citizens, Greece is just like any other European country – you can stay as long as you want, work, or even move here without having to deal with any visa paperwork. Pretty sweet, right?

Visitors from the U.S., Canada, Australia, and the UK

Good news for you too! If you're a citizen of the United States, Canada, Australia, or the UK, you don't need a visa to visit Greece as long as your trip is less than 90 days within a 180-day period. That means if you're coming for a short vacation or even hopping around Europe, you can just book your flight, pack your bags, and go.

But, if you're planning on staying longer than 90 days – maybe you've fallen in love with the islands or can't bring yourself to leave the mainland – you'll need to look into a longer-term visa or residence permit. And trust us, we get it. Greece has a way of making you never want to go home.

Pro tip: Keep an eye on your passport's expiration date. Most countries, including Greece, require your passport to be valid for at least six months beyond your planned departure date. If your passport is cutting it close, it's a good idea to renew it before you head out. Better safe than sorry!

Travelers from Other Countries

If you're not from the EU, U.S., or one of the other visa-exempt countries, don't worry – visiting Greece is still easy. You'll just need to apply for a Schengen Visa before you go. This type of visa allows you to visit Greece and any other Schengen country for up to 90 days within a 180-day period. The process is pretty straightforward, but it's a good idea to apply well in advance, just in case there are any delays.

To apply for a Schengen Visa, you'll need to fill out an application, provide a valid passport, proof of travel insurance, and possibly some extra documentation, like your flight and hotel bookings. You'll also need to pay a fee (around 80 euros, but it varies slightly depending on your country). Once approved, your visa will cover your entire trip, not just Greece, so you can visit other countries in the Schengen Zone while you're here.

Pro tip: Make sure your travel insurance covers medical expenses. Greece, like other Schengen countries, requires that you have insurance with at least €30,000 in coverage. It sounds like a lot, but most standard travel insurance policies meet this requirement.

Long-Term Stays: What if You Want to Stay Longer?

Greece is one of those places where time just seems to fly by. A couple of weeks can quickly turn into a couple of months, and before you know it, you're thinking, "What if I just stay?" If you're planning on a longer adventure or maybe even moving to Greece, you'll need to dig a little deeper into the visa process.

For stays longer than 90 days, non-EU visitors will need to apply for a national visa or a residence permit. This could be for work, study, or even just extended travel. The type of visa you apply for depends on why you're staying, but in general, the process involves filling out forms, providing documentation, and possibly attending an interview at a Greek embassy or consulate.

If you're thinking about working in Greece, the requirements can be a bit more complicated, so it's worth looking into the specifics early. However, if you're just planning to stay a bit longer and soak up the culture, Greece does offer digital nomad visas for remote workers. This relatively new visa makes it easier for people working online to settle in for a while without the stress of needing a full work visa.

ETIAS: Something New for Travelers from Visa-Exempt Countries

There's one more thing to be aware of if you're from a country that doesn't need a visa to visit Greece. Starting in 2025, Greece (along with all Schengen countries) will require citizens of visa-exempt countries to apply for an ETIAS **(European Travel Information and Authorization**

System) before they enter. The ETIAS isn't a visa – it's more like an online registration that helps European authorities keep track of travelers entering the Schengen Zone.

The good news? It's a quick and simple process, similar to applying for an ESTA when traveling to the U.S. You'll fill out an online form, pay a small fee (usually around €7), and you'll get an email confirming your authorization. Once you're approved, your ETIAS will be valid for up to three years or until your passport expires.

So, if you're planning a trip to Greece after 2025, make sure you add ETIAS to your pre-trip to-do list. It's an easy process, but it's something you'll need to do before you fly.

What Happens if You Overstay?

Greece is such an incredible place that we can understand why someone might want to stay forever. But before you settle into island life for the long haul, make sure you're not overstaying your visa or the 90-day limit for visa-free travelers. If you overstay, you could face fines, future travel bans, or even deportation. Definitely not the kind of souvenir you want to take home with you!

If you realize you're about to overstay, it's best to act fast. Contact the local authorities or visit an embassy to see what your options are. In some cases, you might be able to apply for an extension, but it's always better to leave on time and avoid any future headaches.

Climate Conditions: The Best Time to Visit Greece

Planning the perfect trip to Greece? One of the biggest factors to consider is the weather. Greece is a year-round destination, but the climate shifts a bit depending on the time of year and the region you're exploring. Whether you're after sunny beaches, hiking trails, or a stroll through ancient ruins, knowing when to visit can make all the difference. Let's dive into the seasons, so you can choose the best time to enjoy everything this beautiful country has to offer.

The Mediterranean Climate: What to Expect

Greece has a classic Mediterranean climate, which means hot summers, mild winters, and plenty of sunshine. The islands and coastal areas tend to be warmer, while the mainland and northern parts can see a bit more variety in the weather. Regardless of the season, Greece always has something special to offer, so it really depends on what type of experience you're looking for.

Summer (June to August): The High Season

Summer in Greece is what most people imagine when they think of their Greek holiday. This is peak season, especially in popular spots like Santorini, Mykonos, and Crete. From June through August, you can expect long, sunny days with temperatures often hitting around 30-35°C (86-95°F). It's the perfect time for beach lovers and anyone looking to bask in the heat and sunshine.

The sea is warm, the skies are clear, and the islands are bustling with energy. In the Cyclades, you'll experience the famous meltemi winds, which help cool things down a bit, especially in July and August. These winds are strong but refreshing, making them perfect for windsurfing or sailing. If you're not a fan of sweltering heat, these breezes can be a relief, though they can also make some ferry rides a bit choppy!

While summer is undeniably gorgeous, there's no denying it can get crowded. The beaches are packed, the ferries are full, and hotel prices are at their highest. If you're heading to the islands in the summer, book well in advance and prepare for a lively, festive atmosphere.

Pro tip: If you can handle the heat, try visiting Greece in late June or early September. You'll still get those summer vibes, but with fewer crowds and slightly cooler evenings.

Spring (April to May): Warm Days, Cool Nights

Springtime in Greece is nothing short of magical. As the landscape awakens, the hillsides are covered in wildflowers, and the weather starts to warm up, making it one of the best times to visit. From April to May, you'll find mild temperatures ranging from 15-25°C (59-77°F), with plenty of sunshine, but without the intense heat of summer.

This is a fantastic season for sightseeing, especially if you want to explore ancient ruins, hike through olive groves, or wander around charming villages without sweating buckets. It's also a quieter time, so you'll have many places almost to yourself – perfect for those who prefer a slower, more relaxed pace.

While it might be a bit too chilly for swimming (the sea takes a while to warm up), some brave souls take the plunge. By late May, the water starts to become more inviting, and the beaches begin to fill up. Islands like Rhodes, Kos, and Corfu are particularly beautiful in spring, with lush greenery and blooming landscapes.

Pro tip: Easter is a huge celebration in Greece, especially in April. If you visit around this time, you'll get to experience traditional festivals, feasts, and processions that are full of local flavor. Just keep in mind that Easter week can be busy, and prices might spike in certain areas.

Autumn (September to October): The Sweet Spot

For many, autumn is the absolute best time to visit Greece. September is still technically summer in Greece, with temperatures hovering around 25-30°C (77-86°F), but without the overwhelming heat or crowds. The sea remains warm from the summer months, making it an ideal time for swimming, snorkeling, or sailing. It's like having the perks of summer without the hassle.

As you move into October, the weather becomes cooler, especially in the evenings, with temperatures dropping to around 20°C (68°F). The islands become quieter, making this a perfect time to visit if you're seeking a more peaceful escape. You can explore the iconic sights of Santorini, Mykonos, or Naxos without competing with hordes of tourists.

In mainland Greece, autumn is fantastic for outdoor activities like hiking, especially in regions like Pelion, Meteora, or Mount Olympus. The weather is just right for long walks through the countryside, and you'll still get plenty of sunny days, though you might need a light jacket for the cooler nights.

Pro tip: September and October are great months for wine lovers. Its harvest season in Greece, so head to regions like Nemea or Crete for wine festivals, tastings, and tours of local vineyards.

Winter (November to March): Off the Beaten Path

Winter in Greece is often overlooked, but it's actually a wonderful time to experience a different side of the country. While it's not beach weather (unless you love cold water!), there's still plenty to enjoy. The cooler months bring milder temperatures, usually ranging from 10-15°C (50-59°F) in most parts, though it can get colder in the northern regions and mountains.

The islands tend to wind down significantly in the winter, with many hotels and restaurants closing up shop. But if you prefer peace and quiet, winter could be your time to visit. You can wander through towns like Rhodes Old Town or Chania without the tourist buzz, and enjoy more authentic, laid-back interactions with locals.

Winter is also a fantastic time to explore Athens and other major cities. Without the summer heat, you can easily spend your days exploring the Acropolis, the National Archaeological Museum, and the charming neighborhoods of Plaka and Monastiraki. You'll also have the added bonus of off-season prices and more affordable accommodations.

For those who love adventure, Greece even has ski resorts! Mount Parnassos, located near Delphi, is one of the best spots for skiing and snowboarding, offering stunning views of the surrounding countryside. Kalavryta and Vasilitsa are other popular resorts for winter sports enthusiasts.

Pro tip: If you're visiting in winter, pack a bit of everything. While the weather is generally mild, it can be unpredictable. A warm coat and an umbrella are good ideas, especially if you're heading into the mountains.

The Best Time for Your Greek Adventure

So, when is the best time to visit Greece? Well, it really depends on what you want from your trip. For beach lovers and sun seekers, summer is king. But if you're looking to explore the history, culture, and natural beauty of Greece without the heat and crowds, spring and autumn are hard to beat. And for those who love a quieter, more off-the-beaten-path experience, winter holds its own charm.

Whatever time you choose, Greece has something to offer every month of the year. Whether you're diving into the turquoise waters of the Aegean, hiking up ancient trails, or sipping coffee in a cozy taverna, Greece welcomes you with open arms and unforgettable experiences. Just pick the season that speaks to you, and let the magic of Greece unfold.

Chapter Nine

Banking and Currency Exchange: Especially for Tourists and Travelers in Greece

When you're traveling, money matters. From getting cash in the local currency to paying with cards, knowing how to handle banking and currency exchange in Greece will make your trip smoother and stress-free. Don't worry—it's pretty straightforward here, and by the time you're done reading this, you'll be ready to handle your finances like a local. Whether you're wondering where to get the best exchange rates or how to pay for that souvlaki at a food stall, we've got you covered.

Currency in Greece: The Euro (€)

Greece uses the euro (€), which is the common currency across much of Europe. If you're coming from another country within the Eurozone, things will be super easy for you—no need to worry about exchanging your money. For everyone else, you'll need to swap your home currency for euros. Thankfully, there are plenty of ways to do that, and most are pretty convenient.

Bringing Cash with You

It's always smart to bring some cash with you when you travel. That said, don't stress too much about carrying large amounts of cash because ATMs are everywhere in Greece. Still, having at least 50 to 100 euros on hand when you land is a good idea, just in case you need to grab a taxi, buy a coffee, or pay for something small right away.

You can get euros before you leave your home country at a bank or exchange service, but keep in mind that airports and hotel exchange desks often offer poor rates. So, if you're exchanging money before your trip, it's a good idea to shop around for the best deal.

Currency Exchange in Greece: Where to Get the Best Rates

Once you've arrived in Greece, exchanging currency is pretty simple. But like anywhere, some places are better than others when it comes to getting a fair deal. Here are a few options:

1. Banks

Banks are generally a safe bet for currency exchange, offering decent rates and lower fees compared to airport kiosks or touristy exchange offices. You'll find plenty of banks in all major cities and towns, and most are open from around 8:00 AM to 2:00 PM on weekdays (with some staying open later in bigger cities). If you need cash outside of banking hours, ATMs are your best friend.

2. Exchange Offices

If you're in a rush or need to exchange money outside of banking hours, you can always head to a currency exchange office. These are typically found in major cities and tourist hotspots, like Athens, Thessaloniki, and on the islands. However, not all exchange offices are created equal—some offer better rates than others. Always check the exchange rate and fees before handing over your money. A helpful tip is to avoid exchanging money in highly touristy areas like airports, as they tend to charge more.

3. ATMs

ATMs are a convenient way to get cash in Greece. They're everywhere—airports, cities, small towns, and even the islands. Withdrawing euros directly from an ATM usually gives you a better exchange rate than what you'd get at a currency exchange office. However, be mindful of foreign transaction fees that your home bank might charge. Some ATMs in Greece may also charge their own fee, but this varies depending on the bank and your card provider.

To avoid high fees, try to withdraw larger amounts at once instead of making lots of small withdrawals. And don't worry, if you do run out of cash, finding an ATM won't be an issue in most areas.

Pro tip: Stick to ATMs that are part of a bank. ATMs located inside banks or right outside tend to have lower fees than standalone machines, which can sometimes hit you with extra charges.

Using Credit and Debit Cards in Greece

Credit and debit cards are widely accepted in Greece, especially in cities and on the more popular islands. Most restaurants, hotels, and shops will accept major cards like Visa and Mastercard. American Express and Diners Club are less common, so it's good to have a Visa or Mastercard as backup if your main card is AmEx.

For smaller, local businesses—especially in rural areas or at open-air markets—it's wise to carry cash. Some small tavernas, cafés, and street vendors may not take cards, or they might have a minimum spending limit to use one.

When using your card, remember that some merchants may ask if you want to be charged in your home currency (this is known as Dynamic Currency Conversion). While this sounds convenient, it usually means you'll get a less favorable exchange rate, so it's almost always better to opt for being charged in euros.

Pro tip: Before you leave for Greece, let your bank know about your travel plans. This helps avoid any awkward moments where your card gets blocked for suspicious activity while you're in the middle of buying those cute handmade sandals!

Contactless Payments: Tap and Go

Contactless payments are becoming more and more common in Greece, especially in cities like Athens and tourist-heavy islands like Mykonos and Santorini. If your card has a contactless chip, you can tap to pay for small purchases—super easy when you're grabbing a quick snack or drink.

Mobile payment apps like Apple Pay and Google Pay are also gaining traction, so you can leave your wallet behind and pay straight from your phone if you prefer. Just be aware that smaller places, like family-run shops or remote areas, may still prefer cash.

Banking Hours and Services

Greek banks typically open Monday to Friday, from around 8:00 AM to 2:00 PM, with a few branches staying open later in busier areas. Most banks close on weekends and public holidays, so plan ahead if you need to do any in-person banking.

If you do need to visit a bank, the staff are generally helpful, and you'll usually find someone who speaks English, especially in the more tourist-heavy areas. Just remember, lines can get long, especially around midday, so try to go earlier in the morning if you need to exchange money or handle banking tasks.

Traveler's Checks: Are They Still a Thing?

Once upon a time, traveler's checks were a go-to for international travel. These days, however, they're not as widely used or accepted, especially in Greece. You may find a few places willing to cash them, but its more hassle than it's worth. Most travelers prefer to rely on a combination of cash, credit/debit cards, and ATMs to get by. If you're old-school and like the security of traveler's checks, just be prepared for a bit of legwork when trying to cash them.

Security Tips: Keeping Your Money Safe

Like anywhere, it's smart to take a few precautions to keep your money and cards safe while traveling in Greece. Here are a few tips:

- Use ATMs attached to banks rather than standalone machines. These are generally safer and more reliable.
- Carry a mix of cash and cards. Don't rely on just one payment method in case of emergencies.
- Keep an eye on your belongings, especially in busy areas like the Athens metro or popular tourist sites. Pickpocketing can happen in crowded places, so it's a good idea to keep your cash and cards tucked away in a secure spot.
- Divide your money between your wallet and a separate place, like a money belt or a hidden pouch. That way, if you lose one, you still have a backup.

Chapter Ten

Safety and Health Precautions

While Greece is a safe and welcoming destination, it's always smart to keep a few health and safety tips in mind during your travels. Whether you're lounging on a beach, exploring ancient ruins, or hopping between islands, taking a few precautions will ensure your trip is nothing but smooth sailing. Don't worry—this isn't about scaring you, just keeping you informed so you can relax and enjoy every moment.

General Safety: Keeping it Easy and Relaxed

First off, let's clear something up: Greece is considered one of the safest countries in Europe. Crime rates are low, and violent crime is very rare, especially when it comes to tourists. That being said, like in any popular travel destination, petty theft can happen, especially in crowded areas.

When you're wandering through busy streets or catching a ferry to the islands, keep an eye on your belongings. Places like the Athens metro, markets, and tourist-heavy spots like the Acropolis can sometimes attract pickpockets. Keep your wallet, phone, and passport in a secure spot— think a cross-body bag or a money belt if you're feeling extra cautious.

Pro tip: Avoid keeping all your cash and cards in one place. Spread things out a little, so if something does go missing, you're not stuck without access to your money.

Getting Around Safely: Roads, Taxis, and Ferries

Navigating Greece is part of the fun, whether you're driving through the countryside, riding a ferry between islands, or catching a bus in the city. While getting around is generally safe, it's good to know a few tips.

Driving: If you're renting a car, be aware that Greek roads can be narrow, and drivers are sometimes… let's say, enthusiastic. In the cities, traffic can get a little hectic, especially in Athens, so take your time, and don't be afraid to pull over and let locals zoom past if you're feeling overwhelmed. On the islands, renting a scooter or ATV can be a blast, but make sure you wear a helmet and stick to the rules of the road. The roads can be steep and curvy, and sometimes not as well-paved as you'd hope!

Taxis and Rides: Taxis are generally safe and reliable, but make sure to agree on a price or ask the driver to use the meter. Apps like Beat (similar to Uber) are popular in Athens and a few other cities, so you can book a ride from your phone with no surprises.

Ferries: Island-hopping on ferries is one of the highlights of visiting Greece. Ferries are safe and a great way to travel, but it's always a good idea to check the weather before your journey. High winds can sometimes lead to choppy waters or ferry cancellations, so be flexible and allow some cushion time if you're catching a flight or have a tight schedule.

Health Care in Greece: What to Expect

The good news? Greece has excellent healthcare services, and as a tourist, you'll have access to both public and private facilities. You'll find hospitals and clinics in major cities and bigger towns, with pharmacies in just about every village. Pharmacies are well-stocked and staffed with knowledgeable pharmacists who often speak English. If you need medication or over-the-counter remedies, popping into a pharmacy is usually the fastest and easiest option.

Pro tip: Pharmacies in Greece usually display a green cross outside, so they're easy to spot. If you're feeling under the weather or just need something for a headache or sunburn, don't hesitate to pop in.

Travel Insurance: Worth the Peace of Mind

It's always smart to have travel insurance. While you're unlikely to need it, it's reassuring to know that if something does go wrong—whether it's a medical emergency or a missed flight—you're covered. If you're visiting from a European Union country, bring your European Health Insurance

Card (EHIC), which will give you access to necessary medical treatment at a lower cost, or sometimes even for free.

For non-EU travelers, good travel insurance will cover most medical issues and accidents, so make sure you've got a policy in place before you fly. The last thing you want to deal with on vacation is a hefty medical bill!

Staying Healthy: Sun, Water, and Food

Greece's sunny climate is one of the reasons people flock here, but that Mediterranean sun can be intense, especially in the summer months. Whether you're hiking, sightseeing, or lying on the beach, protecting yourself from the sun is crucial.

Sun Protection: Bring sunscreen with you, and apply it generously throughout the day. The Greek sun is no joke, and even if you don't feel like you're burning, it can sneak up on you fast. Don't forget a wide-brimmed hat and sunglasses, and try to seek shade during the peak hours (usually between noon and 3 PM). Staying hydrated is key too, especially when it's hot out, so drink plenty of water throughout the day.

Drinking Water: Speaking of water, in most places in Greece, tap water is perfectly safe to drink. However, on some of the smaller islands, the water can taste a bit salty or have a different mineral content, so most people opt for bottled water, which is affordable and easy to find everywhere. If you're unsure, just ask a local or your hotel—they'll let you know what's best in that area.

Eating Local: One of the absolute joys of visiting Greece is the food! Eating fresh, local dishes is a highlight of any trip. For the most part, the food is clean, safe, and delicious, so you don't need to worry much about food safety. However, if you have a sensitive stomach, it's a good idea to stick to well-cooked meals and avoid street food if it looks like it's been sitting out for a while. Enjoy the salads, grilled meats, and fresh seafood— Greek cuisine is as healthy as it gets!

Emergency Numbers: Just in Case

While it's highly unlikely that you'll need to use it, it's always good to know the emergency number in Greece: **112**. This number works for police, fire, and medical emergencies. If you need help, you can call this number from any phone, and English-speaking operators are available.

For less urgent situations, most hotels, hostels, and Airbnb hosts can help you out. Greeks are known for their hospitality, and if you run into any trouble, don't hesitate to ask for assistance—they'll point you in the right direction with a smile.

How to and What to Pack or Prepare as You Journey to Greece

Packing for a trip to Greece is exciting—you're heading to a land filled with stunning beaches, ancient ruins, charming villages, and lively cities. But with so much variety, you might be wondering: What exactly should you bring? No worries! Packing for Greece doesn't have to be complicated. Whether you're planning a sun-soaked island getaway or exploring historical sites, we've got you covered with this simple, friendly guide.

Clothes: Keep It Light and Comfortable

Let's start with the basics—what to wear. Greece, for the most part, is warm and sunny, so lightweight, breathable clothes are your best bet. Whether you're walking through the streets of Athens or lounging on a beach in Crete, you'll want to feel comfortable and cool.

Summer Months (June to September)

If you're visiting during the summer, expect plenty of sunshine and temperatures that often hover around 30°C (86°F) or higher. Pack plenty of shorts, light dresses, and t-shirts—anything that helps you beat the heat. Swimsuits are a must, especially if you plan to spend time on the islands or by the sea. You'll also want flip-flops or sandals for the beach, but don't forget a pair of sturdy walking shoes or sneakers for exploring cities and archaeological sites. Those cobblestones can be tricky in heels!

Spring and Autumn (April to May, September to October)

If you're traveling in the spring or autumn, the weather is still lovely, but it's a bit cooler, especially in the evenings. Layers are key—bring a light jacket or sweater for the cooler nights and early mornings, but stick to light clothing during the day. You'll still want comfortable shoes for walking, as well as a scarf or shawl that you can easily toss in your bag, just in case the temperature dips.

Winter Months (November to March)

If you're traveling during the winter, keep in mind that Greece can get surprisingly chilly, especially in the northern parts and higher altitudes. You'll need warmer clothing like a jacket, jeans, and long-sleeve shirts. Even on the islands, while it's milder than on the mainland, you'll still want to pack a coat or sweater for those breezy nights.

Pro tip: No matter when you visit, pack something a bit nicer for dinner. Greeks love dressing up a bit in the evenings, so a smart-casual outfit will fit in perfectly if you're heading out for a nice meal or enjoying the nightlife.

Sun Protection: Your Best Friend in Greece

Greece is blessed with sunshine, and while that's one of the many reasons people love visiting, it also means you'll need to be prepared for the sun's intensity.

Start with a good sunscreen (SPF 30 or higher), and make sure to apply it generously throughout the day, especially if you're spending time outdoors. A wide-brimmed hat or a cap is a great idea to keep the sun off your face, and don't forget a pair of sunglasses to protect your eyes. Greece's blue skies and reflective waters can be bright, so good eye protection is a must.

A light, foldable beach towel or sarong is also handy for the beach. They're easy to carry and double as a cover-up when you want to walk to the nearest taverna for a snack.

Pro tip: A reusable water bottle is your friend, especially when you're out and about. Staying hydrated is key, and carrying your own water is a simple way to avoid buying plastic bottles.

Travel Essentials: Don't Forget These

While packing your clothes and beach gear is fun, there are a few other essentials you won't want to leave behind.

Travel Documents

You won't get far without your passport, so double-check that it's packed and valid for at least six months beyond your travel dates. If you're from a country that requires a visa for Greece, make sure you've got that sorted before you leave.

It's also a good idea to print out copies of your flight details, hotel reservations, and travel insurance (just in case you need them) and keep them in a separate place from your passport. You never know when you might need a backup copy.

Power Adapter

In Greece, the standard voltage is 230V, and the plug sockets are Type C and F (the two-round-pin style you find throughout much of Europe). If you're coming from the U.S., UK, or elsewhere, don't forget a universal power adapter to keep your phone, camera, and other devices charged.

Medications and Toiletries

While you can find most basic toiletries in Greece, it's always good to bring your preferred products. Pack a toiletry bag with essentials like toothbrush, toothpaste, shampoo, and razor, but don't overdo it—most items are easy to buy locally if you run out.

If you take any prescription medications, make sure you bring enough for the entire trip, as well as the prescriptions in case you need to refill them. A small first aid kit with Band-Aids, pain relievers, and some antihistamines for allergies is also a smart idea. You never know when you might need something, especially if you're out hiking or exploring remote areas.

Gadgets and Gear: Capture the Moment

You'll want to capture those gorgeous sunsets and ancient ruins, so don't forget your camera or smartphone! If you're a photography buff, bring along a portable charger to keep your devices powered while you're out adventuring. Don't forget an extra memory card if you plan on taking a lot of photos.

For those who love the water, a waterproof phone case or camera is a fun addition. Greece has some of the clearest waters in Europe, and you'll want to snap a few underwater shots while snorkeling or swimming.

If you're planning on hiking or exploring the islands by foot, a daypack is a must. It's the perfect size for carrying your essentials—water, sunscreen, snacks, and camera—without being bulky.

Useful Extras: Packing for Convenience

Here are a few more little things that can make a big difference during your trip:

- **Portable laundry bag:** Perfect for keeping dirty clothes separate, especially if you're moving around between islands or cities.
- **Travel-sized hand sanitizer:** Greece is clean, but it's always handy to have sanitizer when you're on the go.
- **Portable fan or cooling towel:** If you're visiting in the summer, this can be a lifesaver on those extra hot days.
- **Books or an e-reader:** Long ferry rides between islands are a great time to relax with a good book.

Map of Greece

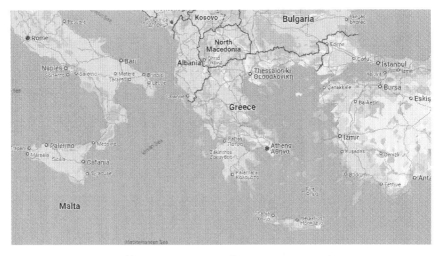

https://maps.app.goo.gl/n13zjpz28ZnoWbsd7

Map of Cheap Hotels in Greece

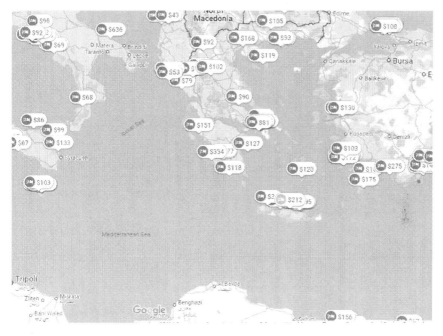

https://maps.app.goo.gl/RHUoUpd55BNQ7wpW9

212

Map of Where to Eat in Greece

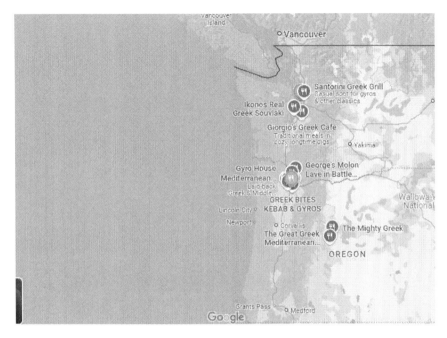

https://maps.app.goo.gl/6sWKVZCJohCqb3KW8

Map of Beaches in Greece

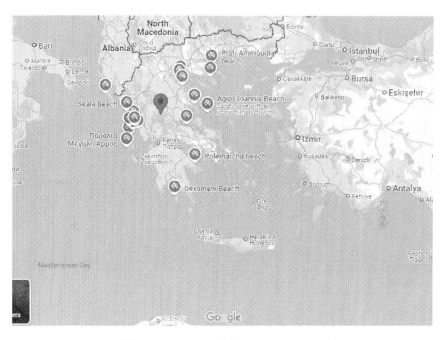

https://maps.app.goo.gl/MNyarBo3tpoPNfCC8

Map of Museums in Greece

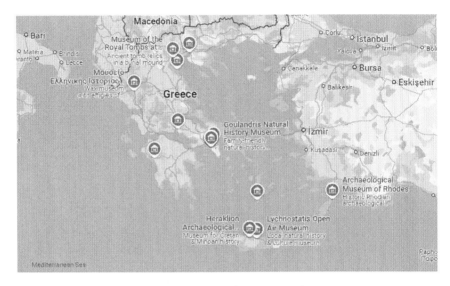

https://maps.app.goo.gl/Q5gasv9XnhQc9SWZ9

Map of where to Hike in and Around Greece

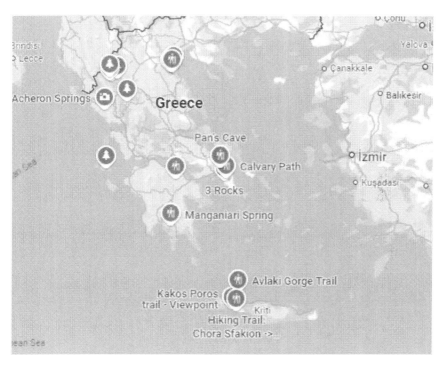

https://maps.app.goo.gl/cwKyZCGCDFUoGAyi8

Map of Greece's Historic sites

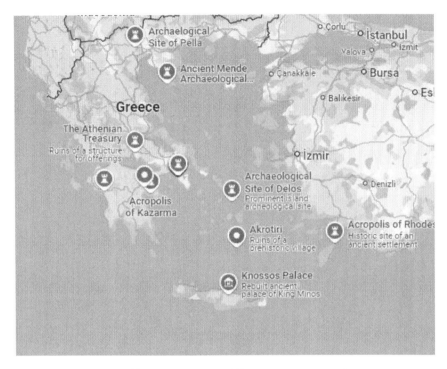

https://maps.app.goo.gl/fzAvV5x98QGsa3tk6

Map of Greece's Best Shopping Spots

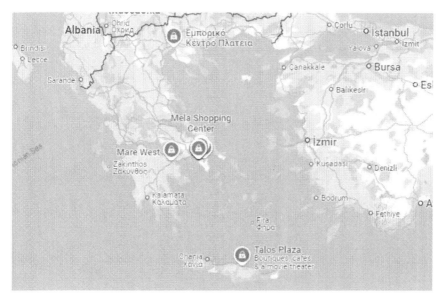

https://maps.app.goo.gl/PbPyuvoVcoqYbeo99

Map of Public Transportation in Greece

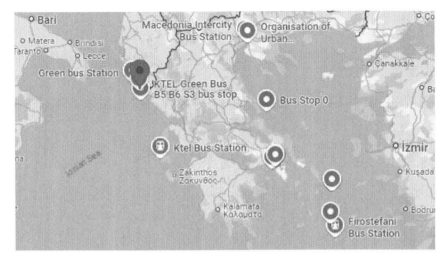

https://maps.app.goo.gl/peMFLP5tnzeBNW1A6

Map of Parks and Gardens in Greece

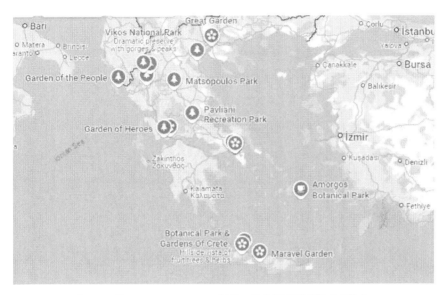

https://maps.app.goo.gl/GzrR66RZSSTxkjPk8

SAYING GOOD BYE TO GREECE

Importantly, do not forget to leave a little space in your bag for those *souvenirs* you will be bringing back!

In addition, kindly help us to give an *honest review* for this book. We appreciate you.

Safe travels!

Made in the USA
Las Vegas, NV
04 December 2024

13357311R00122